The Big Book of
Words
That Sell

1200 Words and Phrases That Every Salesperson and Marketer Should Know and Use

Robert W. Bly

Skyhorse Publishing

To Michael Campbell

Skyhorse Publishing books may be purchased in bulk at special discounts for sales promotion, corporate gifts, fund-raising, or educational purposes. Special editions can also be created to specifications. For details, contact the Special Sales Department, Skyhorse Publishing, 307 West 36th Street, 11th Floor, New York, NY 10018 or info@skyhorsepublishing.com.

Skyhorse® and Skyhorse Publishing® are registered trademarks of Skyhorse Publishing, Inc.®, a Delaware corporation.

Visit our website at www.skyhorsepublishing.com.

10 9 8 7 6 5 4

Library of Congress Cataloging-in-Publication Data is available on file.

Cover design by Qualcom Designs

ISBN: 978-1-5107-4175-1
Ebook ISBN: 978-1-5107-4176-8

Printed in China

Acknowledgments

I want to thank my literary agent, Bob Diforio, for his usual fine work in finding a home for this book. Thanks also to my editor, Michael Campbell, for his extraordinary gift of time and patience enabling me to write what turned out to be a much more difficult book than I originally anticipated—thanks to his sharp editing, a much better book, too.

In addition, I owe a debt of gratitude to the dozens of copywriters, salespeople, entrepreneurs, speakers, writers, advertising agencies, and marketers whose most potent persuasive phrases made their way into this book. I can't name them all, but you know who you are, folks.

"A good advertisement is one which sells the product without draw-ing attention to itself. It should rivet the reader's attention on the product. It is the professional duty of the advertising agent to conceal his artifice."

—*David Ogilvy,* Confessions of an Advertising Man

Table of Contents

Introduction

The rise of the web has created an increased demand for people who can persuade others with words. Selling on the Internet is steadily approaching a trillion-dollar market; in 2017, global e-commerce revenues were $360 billion. And that doesn't include all the other selling that takes place every day, both online and offline—from infomercials offering ab machines to car salespeople trying to sell more autos, and even Jehovah's Witnesses persuading people to join their religion by going door to door. The *New York Times* reports that the average city dweller sees up to 5,000 ad messages per day, as amazing as that sounds. In 2017, U.S. businesses spent $197 billion on advertising.

What are the secrets to persuading others in print, on the screen, or in person using words? One of the most potent is the use of the trigger words and phrases that motivate people, command attention, and persuade them to buy your product or service. As an old radio commercial for a mail-order vocabulary course once noted: "People judge you by the words you use." Eventually, everybody has access to the same technology. So once everyone's technologically up-to-date, the one thing remaining that separates your marketing campaign from your competitors' is the words you use.

The Big Book of Words That Sell is your guide to many of the world's most persuasive words and phrases—words that can affect how readers or listeners think, feel, and act—and influence what they believe and do. After reading this book, you will be able to:

- Sell virtually any product or service.
- Convince people to agree with your point of view.
- Select just the right words for every marketing campaign.
- Transform tepid writing into sparkling and persuasive prose.
- Improve click-throughs, conversions rates, and other performance metrics.
- Find ready-to-use phrases and sentences that fit your ad perfectly.
- Use language that has been proven to sell.
- Choose the right keywords and keyword phrases.

The format is simple. The book has hundreds of entries organized by category as shown in the table of contents. The words and phrases are grouped in chapters according to application, e.g., words that create a sense of urgency, words that announce a new product, or ones that grab the reader's attention. Each entry is a persuasive word or phrase in boldface, followed by an example, in italics, of its use. Many of the examples are from actual ads, websites, and other copy and content, both digital and offline. Each section has a short introduction explaining the theme or concept the words in the section are used to communicate, or the communications goal their use aims to achieve.

The book serves several audiences, and because you are reading it, I am guessing you fall into one or more of the following categories:

- Selling products and services on the Internet has become the biggest entrepreneurial business opportunity of the 21st century. Therefore, the book has wide appeal to online entrepreneurs, of which GreatMailingLists.com estimates there are 18.5 million nationwide. And half of all ad spend today is digital.[1]

---

1   https://blog.hubspot.com/news-trends/digital-ad-spend-to-surpass-tv-print-2019.

- The book is also ideal for aspiring Internet marketing entrepreneurs as well as those who already have an online business but want to increase their sales. SmallBusinessBible.org reports that the Internet today is a huge marketplace with over a billion visitors going online every day, and that according to research surveys conducted, there are millions of businesses and stores online with literally hundreds of thousands of web pages—a large number of which require persuasive writing.
- The book is also a valuable resource for those who sell for a living: sales managers, professional sales representatives, ad agencies, PR firms, copywriters, content writers, public relations professionals, marketing managers, brand managers, product managers, account executives, telemarketers, and multilevel marketers. Advertising and marketing professionals as well as salespeople are held accountable for results today, and these tested words and phrases can help make your numbers better and produce more sales and profits.
- In addition, virtually every small business sells a product or service. The book will give these business owners and managers the vocabulary they need for more effective marketing, selling, and communication.
- Even if you are not by profession in sales or marketing, you may find *The Big Book of Words That Sell* interesting—even helpful. There are endless situations that require persuasion but have nothing to do with marketing, advertising, or selling a product or service—everything from getting more members to attend your monthly club meetings to asking your landlord not to raise the rent.

A Few More Words about the Words in This Book

You may notice that almost all of the words and phrases in this book are short, simple, and easy to understand. Plain English. Not highfalutin language. That's deliberate. And here's why.

Copywriters and other writers long ago discovered that most adults read at the level of elementary school students. Today, English skills, literacy, and the reading skills of your prospects are, if anything, declining rather than improving.

There are many reasons. I won't go into most of them here. But obviously, the web has trained people to read increasingly shorter and simpler text. Getting through and comprehending a 200-page book requires greater thought and attention span than reading a 200-word blog post.

We know from long experience that for our copy to work, it has to be understood. In fact, Ralph Waldo Emerson said it is not enough to write to be understood; you have to write so clearly and simply that your readers cannot possibly misunderstand you. And that is not always easy to achieve. As Terry C. Smith, former communications manager at Westinghouse has noted, "Easy reading is hard writing."

Years ago, I interviewed the CEO of a large advertising agency to gather information for a book I was writing on careers in advertising and other industries. In the course of our conversation, this CEO complained to me of the lack of basic writing skills in the young people who sought employment with his agency.

"We get people who have college degrees," he said, "and they can't write an English sentence."

Functional illiteracy is nothing new, but among advertising people? I was skeptical until I turned on the television that evening and heard a commercial describing a new television series as "the most unique show of the season." This seems a strange claim to make, since *unique* means "one of a kind," and it is therefore impossible for anything to be the most unique. Or *very* unique, or *quite* unique, or *somewhat* unique, or even, as one advertising executive used the phrase modestly, *a little* unique. Yes, when selling, there are times when deliberate redundancy works well. But to break the rules with good effect, you have to know the rules first. And many people don't. That's a problem this book aims to help correct for you.

TV is not the only advertising medium guilty of turning advertising copy into what E.B. White, coauthor of *The Elements of Style,* called "the language of mutilation." A Detroit automobile manufacturer once based an ad campaign around the theme "new innovations"—which may lead one to believe that there can be such a thing as an *old* innovation. Again, you can use "new innovations" and be deliberately redundant in sales and marketing writing. The key is to do it sparingly and know when it is appropriate to do so.

One of my clients, normally an articulate and intelligent marketer, changed some ad copy I had written for one of their products, a wire splint that helps keep loose teeth in place. The advertiser decided that what the product *really* did was "to stabilize mobile dentition."

Dentition is what you brush with Crest. And if someone should punch you in the dentition, my client believes that the dentition may become mobile, rather than merely loose. (If they fall out, the dentition fairy may deposit some "monetary compensation" under your pillow.)

"I'm chagrined at the decline in the writing skills of college graduates," Hugh Farrell, then president of Hammond Farrell, Inc., a New York business-to-business advertising agency, told me in another interview for my book. "Roughly half of the cover letters accompanying résumés that cross my desk contain errors, and I don't think that was true fifteen years ago. And good writing is important, even with account people. If a person can't write a lucid, clear, correct report, he or she shouldn't be in this business."

Jargon, double-talk, and weak, watered-down prose proliferate in copy and content but perhaps are nowhere more prevalent than in business-to-business marketing. A brochure for a storage silo informs us that material is "gravimetrically conveyed"—not dumped. Sony's advertisement for my pocket minicassette recorder explains that my device captured Burt Manning's grievance so perfectly because "a counter-inertial flywheel keeps the tape speed constant."

True perhaps, but did I really need to know this? And, of course, every system, product, and service now sold to business is said to be "cost-effective" or provide a lower "total cost of ownership." How refreshing it would be to read of a product that was inexpensive, low in price, or just plain cheap!

I've always maintained that good writing is clear and conversational . . . but there are many marketers who apparently disagree. For instance, here's an excerpt from a brochure promoting a business conference on *Buying and Selling eContent:*

> Instead of building universal, definitive taxonomies, information architects are finding there is a tremendous benefit to creating un-taxonomized miscellaneous pools of enriched data objects so that users can sort and organize to suit their own peculiar needs . . . [resulting in] information systems that are far more contextualized.

I call this example "What did he say?" It's pretentious, laden with jargon, and it's not how people talk. My fellow copywriter Steve Slaunwhite comments: "This is a case of trying to impress, rather than express. The problem is, it does neither."

Certainly, such obfuscation has not always been embraced by English-speaking people. Winston Churchill, faced with Hitler's armed forces, said to Americans, "Give us the tools and we will do the job." He did *not* say: "Aid our organization in the procurement of the necessary equipment and we will in turn implement the program to accomplish its planned objectives."

Socialist Susan Brownmiller described jargon as "language more complex than the idea it serves to communicate." Sy Sperling, founder of The Hair Club for Men, says simple ideas are the best ideas—and that goes for communicating ideas in writing, too.

Happily, academia has now recognized the problem and is working toward a solution. *Forbes* reports that undergraduate engineering students at MIT will be required to take a course in English composition. The *New York Times* notes that the number of writing courses at colleges throughout the nation is now on the rise—and that American corporations are now spending more than $3 billion a year teaching employees how to write clearly.

As a result of improved education, the next generation of college graduates should be able to write sales letters and reports that buyers and managers can understand. Meanwhile, those of us who may never see the inside of a classroom again would do well to heed this bit of advice from E.B. White: "When you have said something, make sure you have said it. The chances of your having said it are only fair."

This book gives you a wide range of short, simple words and phrases that can help you get your message across, gain the prospect's attention, and get him or her interested in what you are selling and ultimately buy it—whether it's a new digital watch to a consumer or a business idea to your client.

One other thing: some words appear multiple times in the book and in more than one section, because the words have multiple applications. For instance, the word "why" can be used to introduce a list of product benefits, e.g., "7 reasons why TV commercial directors prefer Unilux strobe lighting." In another phrasing, "why" can explain an idea, fact, opinion, or concept to the reader, e.g., "Why every man hopes his first child will be a boy."

I do have one favor to ask: if you have a favorite selling phrase, why not send it to me so I can share it with readers of the next edition of this book? You can email me at rwbly@bly.com. I welcome your contributions and feedback. Thanks!

CHAPTER 1

Targeting and Engaging Audiences

The most important thing you can do to increase your marketing results is to find and reach the right audience—the ideal buyers for your offer. The more accurately you target your marketing to the needs, interests, desires, and problems of the target market, the more sales you will make. For instance, if you are a user of email marketing and direct mail, you can rent digital and postal lists that reach potential customers in thousands of different markets. In organic search, using long-tail keyword phrases (e.g., "restored 1985 Pontiac Star Chief with automatic transmission") targets your prospect better than "cars."

Also, the narrower the audience your copy targets, the higher the readership and response. For that reason, you may want to segment your e-newsletter, mailings, banner ads, and other promotions into multiple audience-specific promotions, targeted for maximum appeal to each group.

For example, one company I worked with had eight vertical industries—and produced eight separate e-newsletters every other month with links to industry-specific news, events, and other pertinent information.

Use links on your home page to segment multiple audiences. Dell Computer used this strategy effectively with links for consumers, small, medium, and large businesses, and public institutions such as health care and the federal government. Your ads, collateral, e-newsletters, postcards, and direct mail can then drive prospects to market-specific pages.

Getting your message across to multiple audiences on a budget isn't difficult. Look for opportunities for ads and collateral to be easily modified to each audience (e.g., swapping out a picture of a field for farmers in the agricultural market for a photo of an Air Force jet for defense marketing). Consider cost-effective alternatives that are also easily targeted to specific markets, such as banner and online ads, and search engine optimization.

Targeting the audience means knowing who the ideal prospects are for your product or proposition, and then writing copy that lets them *know* they are the ones to whom you are directing your message; this is one of the most effective ways ever devised of gaining the reader's attention, interest, and response.

For instance, if you are advertising an expensive new stationary exercise bicycle to help people recover from injury or surgery—e.g., a knee replacement—who is your target audience? Patients? Physical therapy centers? Knee surgeons who want to improve patient outcomes? Independent physical therapists who come to the patient's home?

When you say who the ad or product is for, those people will sit up and pay attention. When the ad clearly identifies the target market, the people you want to read it are more likely to do so.

There is an old formula for persuasive writing success called WIIFM, which stands for "What's in it for me?" Audience engagement among your target market is strongest when the product or service does something for them, gives them an advantage, solves a pressing problem, or delivers a desired benefit.

Going back to our stationary exercise bicycle, the knee surgeon may buy one to ensure that a greater percentage of his patients get well faster.

Doing so improves patient health and satisfaction and may increase the doctor's insurance reimbursement. Selling it direct to patients as a home exercise bike saves the patient time by eliminating the need to drive back and forth to the doctor or physical therapist every time the patient wants to exercise his or her recovering knee. The physical therapist wants the best and most modern rehab equipment available. It impresses patients and referring physicians and also gets patients better results in less time.

As noted, we also know from long experience that the narrower you target your copy, the more persuasive and effective your writing will be. Some businesspeople hesitate to make their target market too narrow. But here's what we find: the narrower your target market, yes, the fewer prospects you have for your product or service, but *the more money they will pay for it*. Consumers will pay a premium price for products they perceive are tailored to their specific needs, concerns, and problems. Therefore, you can make greater revenues by serving fewer customers or clients, because by targeting, you attract the most serious buyers who will pay the most dollars. So your closing rate on the sale is improved, and your average order has a higher dollar value. As the publisher of the *50 Plus Monthly* newspaper in Morris County, NJ, notes, "Targeted advertising strengthens sales."[2]

Identify Your Target Market

The first step in targeting your market is to identify and clearly define who that target market is.

In some cases, this is obvious and easy. If you are selling maternity clothing, your target market is pregnant women.

But say you are selling reconditioned classic cars that have been restored to their original condition.

You could say the audience is simply people who like classic cars. But restored classic cars are expensive, depending on year and model.

---

2   *50 Plus Monthly*, March 2019, p. 10.

For that reason, many classic car dealers specifically target doctors and dentists. These high-income professions qualify as prospects by being able to afford a classic car. You might want to target Lexus owners, but local Lexus dealers most likely would be unwilling to share their customer list with you. However, you can easily reach dentists, doctors, and other high-income individuals in your zip code and nearby areas.

A car rental company in Florida—not Alamo—rented cars only by the week, not by the day. Because you had to buy a week's rental, their gross was bigger on each customer, and in return for the bigger spend, the company set the rates so that the per day cost was actually *lower* than their competitors who rented primarily by the day.

Who would be the car rental company's ideal target market? Perhaps vacationers to Disney? Teens on spring break? Actually, the most responsive target market turned out to be Florida condo owners. These people, mainly snowbirds and retirees, would stay for weeks at a time, so the weekly billing appealed to them—especially because the more weeks they rented, the bigger the discount.

Say you work for an industrial gas manufacturer and you are writing a white paper on tips for handling compressed cylinder gas. Are you targeting plant managers or plant operators? Plant managers might be more interested in cylinder inventory and control, while plant operators want nuts-and-bolts tips for safe handling of the cylinders. A CFO would want to look at reducing costly gas cylinder accidents and better cylinder inventory control, while the CEO might be concerned about liability.

The following language can be used to identify and engage your target audience:

A special invitation to/for
A special invitation to the hero of American business.

Are you ever _____?
Are you ever tongue-tied at parties?

Aspiring

Announcing an "Apprenticeship Program" for Aspiring Millionaires.

Attention

Attention: All Charter Life Insurance Policy holders.

Available for, available only for

Available for your spouse and other family members.

Calling, calling all

Calling All Organic Gardeners to Try One of the Greatest Organic Gardening Guides Ever Written . . . for 15 Days Free!

Dear _____

Dear Music Lover:

Do you, don't you

Don't you just enjoy . . . being home?

Do you have? Do you know? Do you do?

Do you have a secret fear of losing your job?

Does?

Does your child ever embarrass you?

Especially for you

If you drive in harsh winters with lots of snow and ice, the new all-wheel Nissan was designed especially for you.

Every _____ over age _____

The love-making video every man over 60 should watch.

Fellow

Dear Fellow Gardener,

For _____

For the woman who is older than she looks.

For _____ only

For serious golfers only.

For the _____ lover

For the World War II history lover.

Have you?

Have YOU any of these symptoms of nervous exhaustion?

If you

If you love music, you'll love our magazine.

If you are a _____

If you are a dog person, this is something you'll want to know more about.

Just for you

Just for you: up to 85% off every course!

Members

Free gift for new and renewing members.

Men's Extra Wide Shoes

Men's Extra Wide Shoes—EEE—EEEEEE—FREE catalog from Hancock Shoes.

Mistakes

Do you make these mistakes in English?

Perfect for _____

Perfect for meat lovers who crave a substantial knife at mealtime.

Seniors, older Americans

Legal needs of older Americans.

Serious, avid

For avid coin collectors.

A special offer

A special offer for men and women who did not go to college.

Thinking about _____?

Thinking about going solar?

This is for you

Music lovers—this is for you.

To _____

To every grandmother in America.

Want, want to

To people who want to write—but can't get started.

Wanted

Men wanted for hazardous journey.

We're looking for

We're looking for people to write children's books.

What in the world

What in the world is wrong with me?

Who else?

Who else wants a whiter smile—with no trips to the dentist?

You can make

You can make big money in real estate right now.

Young and old

Easter basket goodies for young and old!

Trigger a Receptive Attitude

"Triggering a receptive attitude" means the reader is at least somewhat open to whatever information, opinion, point of view, or argument he expects you to present. He doesn't necessarily believe it yet. But he is willing to listen.

The trick to ramping up reader receptivity to the next level is a simple principle first articulated by master copywriter Clayton Makepeace: "Enter into the conversation the reader is already having in his mind." What it means is if your statements are congruent with the reader's beliefs and thoughts, you have a better chance of his receiving and believing your message.

For instance, in option trading, marketers of seminars, courses, books, and software promise huge profits. But so many consumers who buy these programs find they are difficult to use, and the courses don't make them easy money as promised. So when you want to talk to them about your option trading system and how much money it can make, their receptivity plummets and skepticism soars, and your message is likely not well received.

So a marketer of option software tried a different approach. His headline was "Why Most Option Trading Systems Don't Work . . . and Never Will." Immediately, receptivity rises and their skepticism is on its way out. Why? Because your words resonate with the exact thought—"these products don't work"—that pops into their minds whenever they hear "option trading system." Instead of arguing with the prospect, you are acknowledging the thought already in their minds—and that's one of the most powerful ways of triggering a receptive attitude.

You can trigger a receptive attitude in your audience by using language like:

Aim high
Aim high. Reach for new horizons.

Are they, are we?
Are they being promoted right over your head?

Avoid unpleasant surprises
How to avoid an unpleasant surprise audit from the IRS.

Better
Better than Botox.

Bright
It takes a bright and sparkling flavor to attract children!

Celebrate
Celebrate President's Day!

Chosen for you, recommended just for you
Based on the places you've dined, these spots were chosen just for you.

Christmas in July
Christmas in July Weekly Specials.

Could this be?
Could this be the greatest weight loss trick ever discovered?

Dimensions
New 3-D Vision Microscope Adds Exciting New Dimensions to Mineralogy!

Dreaming, dream, dream come true
Dreaming of Italy?

Everything you need
Everything you need to keep your roses healthy and beautiful.

Exclusive, exclusively
Auto insurance exclusively for AARP members is affordable for seniors who still drive.

Family values
Disney—family values.

Friendly
Fly the friendly skies of United Airlines.

Fun
FUN with Chemcraft.

Get more
Angel cardholders get more!

Good news
Good news for homeowners who are under water.

Healthy, health
Have healthy teeth and gums for life.

Help, help for you
When I need help, Life Alert is always there.

Indulge, indulge yourself.

Indulge yourself . . . with Belgian chocolates.

It's not your fault.

If you don't have enough money to retire, it's not your fault.

Just a _____

Just a dollar a day can change the life of a child in need.

Keeps the doctor away

A multivitamin a day keeps the doctor away.

Life-changing

The life-changing benefits of an oxygen chamber.

Made only by

REAL Kiddie-Jars are made only by White.

Mix and match

Mix and match 4 select floribundas for ONLY $21.98 each.

My gift to you, our gift to you

Yours FREE—my gift to you.

Never _____

Never have a lawn full of weeds again!

Number one

How to be Number One.

One simple thing

You only have to do just this one simple thing to lose fat and pack on lean muscle!

Peace of mind

Stay connected to the network with greater peace of mind.

Personal

Your personal emergency device needs to work on the go.

Raise

Raise venture capital without losing equity.

Recommended just for you

Recommended just for you—the Sear House Grill.

Scare, scarcity

Own these scarce collector classics!

Status

Classic Trees of Presidential Status.

Straight talk

Some straight talk about earning extra income.

Tailored, tailor

With so many features and options, we can tailor a system that's right for you.

That's right for you

With so many features and options, we can tailor a system that's right for you.

What's not to like?

Free wax and buff with every car wash—what's not to like?

Who else

Who else wants a beautiful garden?

With a little luck

With a little luck, you may be able to retire by age 50 or sooner.

Within easy reach

Now your goals are within easy reach.

Worry no more

Worry no more about shortages, world crises, shutdown, rising prices, future inflations!

You can be sure

You can be sure if it's Westinghouse.

You may have already won

You may have already won the Grand Prize.

You've probably heard

You've probably heard a thing or two about the future of the automotive industry.

Lure the Prospect into the Copy

Think of the reader as a fish. Your words need to "hook" him—or he won't keep reading. Certain words and phrases act as "bait" for the hook; those words and phrases can successfully lure your readers to continue reading (Fig. 1). The following are among the most effective strategies for luring readers into your copy:

- Arouse curiosity.
- Make a big promise.
- Make a great offer such as a free gift.
- Present a fascinating fact.
- Tell readers something they do not know.

- Tell readers something they already know.
- Write a strong title or headline.
- Warn them of danger.
- Appeal to greed.
- Appeal to guilt.
- Appeal to fear.
- Promise them something exclusive or special.
- Ask a question to which their answer will be "yes."
- Create a sense of urgency.

These words and phrases do that:

Acquired at considerable risk

Collectible gold coins acquired at considerable risk to expert divers.

Announcing

Announcing Armstrong Acoustical Fire Guard—a totally new method of installing rated fire protection at substantially lower cost.

Are you?

Are you between the ages of 45 and 74?

Banish

Banish constipation, bloating, and other digestive problems.

Catch

Skittles: catch the rainbow.

Conquer, conquered

I conquered horse racing after I discovered the supreme secret.

Do you have?

Do You Have Any of These Symptoms of Depression?

Do you know?

Do you know how to find a lawyer if you suddenly need one right away?

Don't

Don't buy furniture today!

Enjoy

Enjoy more face time with friends and family.

Find

Find your favorites—check out these new additions . . .

Fresh look

It's time to take a fresh look at today's France.

Get them while they last

New inventory of 20-year old single-malt Scotch—get a bottle or two while they last.

Great _____ aren't made overnight

Great wrought-iron beds aren't made overnight, but painstakingly crafted by expert ironsmiths.

How come?

How Come Some People Can Walk Up to a Blackjack Table and Always Walk Away a Winner?

How do you?

How do you grow $1,000 worth of food in a garden this small?

How to

How to keep your products pure in the pharmaceutical plant.

Ideas

Ideas for a quick-service restaurant.

Imagine

Imagine Harry and me advertising our PEARS in Fortune!

Inside

Inside: a special offer for homeowners in New Jersey.

Is this the end of _____?

Is This the End of . . . Overeating?

Just in time

You're just in time to see the new models of the Lexus RX.

Killer

The Dance-to-Your-Phone is a killer app and a big hit at parties.

Look no further

Seeking an end to your money problems? Look no further!

Master

Master the skill of network administration.

Memorable

7 memorable songs from Broadway—and what makes them great.

Missing piece

Is mindfulness the missing piece to wellness?

Mr. X

Meet Mr. X, the world's top option trader.

Not one person in a thousand

Pears so rare, not one person in a thousand has ever tasted them.

On sale

South America on sale.

Others have paid

Others have paid $3,000 less for beautiful diamond earrings like these.

Questions to ask

7 Questions to Ask Before You Hire a Collection Agency . . . And One Good Answer to Each.

Quiz

Quiz: Are you an introvert or an extrovert?

Read this

Read this or DIE.

Remember, remembered

The 75 photos Ansel Adams wanted to be remembered by.

Revealed, reveals

David Gardener reveals a brand-new stock pick.

Secret

The secret to richer, moister chocolate cake.

The curse

The curse of too much money!

What's wrong?

What's wrong with this picture?

Which of these, which

Which of these best-sellers do you want—for only $1 each?

Who ever heard of?

Who ever heard of losing weight and enjoying 3 delicious meals a day at the same time?

Why haven't _____ been told these facts?

Why haven't TV owners been told these facts?

State an Analogy

An analogy describes a thing that is comparable to another thing in significant respects. Typically, one of the things is known and familiar while the other is new and unfamiliar. Using an analogy makes it easier for the reader to quickly understand and get a mental image of the unfamiliar new thing. Two particular types of analogies are similes and metaphors. Similes use "as" and "like" to make a direct comparison between one thing and another, while metaphors substitute one thing for another to make an implied comparison. These keywords set up imagery as a tool to sell your product.

As

Is IBM's Watson as smart as a professional chess champion?

Like, it's like

Winston tastes good like a cigarette should!

Look like

So large and lush, they make store-bought grapes look like birdseed.

Man's best friend

A Lincoln SUV is a man's best friend.

Steel Trap

How to Develop a Mind Like a Steel Trap.

The next best thing to _____

It's the next best thing to having a live-in maid.

The Rolls-Royce of _____

The Rolls-Royce of air conditioners.

Ticking time bomb

Are your variable annuities a ticking time bomb in your retirement portfolio?

Why some foods "explode"

Why some foods explode in your stomach.

Winning, win

Winning the race to the digital economy by cracking the code of the gender gap.

Arouse Curiosity

If you can arouse curiosity, people will keep reading. A classic example is from the direct mail promotion "What never to eat on an airplane." You have to tear open the envelope and read the enclosed material, because if you ever travel by air, you want to know which airline food you should avoid. Kindle readers' curiosity with language like:

Are these

Owning a Subway franchise—are these your questions?

Are you aware, are you prepared?

Are you prepared for retirement's 4 stages?

Can you name them all?

Seven ways to eliminate joint pain. Can you name them all?

Confessions

Confessions of a disbarred lawyer.

Confidential

For a confidential review, please call me today.

Could this be?

Could this be the most important arthritis breakthrough ever discovered?

Dilemma

A dilemma for many nonprofits.

Fantastic

This Fantastic Secret Turned My Life Around and Made Me Rich.

Here's why

Stocks repurchased by the companies that issue them often rise substantially in share price. Here's why . . .

Hidden

Hidden behind these gates . . .

How fast is _____

How fast is Google changing its advertising policies?

How to

How to Increase Your Standard of Living without Changing Jobs

Insider, insiders

How you can legally profit from "insider information" on the stock market.

Little-known

New FREE Special Report Reveals Little-Known Strategy Millionaires Use to Keep Wealth in Their Hands—and Out of Uncle Sam's.

Mistakes

The 5 most costly mistakes in business. How many are you making right now?

Mystery

Mystery of the Vanishing Hills.

Price tag

Can you put a price tag on happiness?

Secrets

The happiest millionaire around teaches others his secrets.

Suppose

Suppose this happened on YOUR wedding day!

Undercover

Undercover investigation leads to 14 counts of animal cruelty.

What you don't know

What you don't know about corporate law could expose you to personal liability.

What's working

What's working in direct mail.

Why

Why haven't more smart-phone owners been told these facts?

Why in the world
Why in the world would you want to read this ad any further knowing it might cost you $100 at the very least?

Wonder, wonders, ever wonder
Wonder why European men are such great lovers?

X
Learn real estate investing from "Mr. X," North America's most successful house flipper.

You only need _____
You only need 3 ingredients for a great workplace.

You're missing out
You're missing out on new developments in childhood education.

Move Reader Emotionally

There is a long debate in advertising as to which motivates customers more effectively: emotion or logic. Long experience shows that both can work, but of the two, emotional copy usually outperforms straightforward facts. The best strategy is a one-two combination: use emotion to convince the prospect to purchase, then follow it up with facts to reinforce the purchase decision and prevent buyer's remorse.

Conjure emotion with terms like these:

Ambitious, ambition
Ambition doesn't wait.

Back-breaking
No more back-breaking garden chores for ME—yet ours is now the showplace of the neighborhood!

Beat

How to beat high real estate commission rates.

Beg

Top NYC doctors beg Americans to throw this vegetable away.

Call back

Call back these great moments at the opera.

Celebrate

Celebrate love! 20% off select Valentine's Day Items.

Defy

Defy all the excuses.

Don't miss

Don't miss winter teas at Brookgreen Gardens.

Dreams

Dreams do come true.

Enchantment, enchanting

This is New Mexico, the Land of Enchantment.

Fall in love

Jewelry styles you'll fall in love with.

Fed up

Fed up working a dead-end job with low pay?

Garbage

Is the liberal media feeding you a steady diet of pure garbage?

Glory

The glory of the upward path.

Government, big government

What has the government done for you lately?

Hate

Where the women you hate have their hair done.

Heart

Home is where our heart is.

Hell

That's a hell of a way to run a railroad!

Hope

Why does every man hope his first child will be a boy?

How I learned to love

How I learned to relax and love investing.

If you were

If you were given $400,000 to spend—isn't this the kind of vacation home you would own?

Lies; lies, lies, lies

The governor's campaign promises: lies, lies, lies.

Looking up

Lisbon's looking up.

Love

The skin you love to touch.

Missing out

You're missing out on new development in childhood education.

Most intelligent way

The most intelligent way to shop for a second car.

Peace of mind

The Sloman Shield home security system gives you greater peace of mind.

Precious

Too precious not to protect from mosquitoes & ticks.

Protect

Protect your family with up to $100,000 in affordable life insurance.

Quit work

To men who want to quit work someday.

Remember when?

Remember when you could have picked up Amazon, Microsoft, or Google stock for a song—and didn't?

Rip-offs

Avoid rip-offs. Call Samuels Siding today and save!

Rob

How to rob race tracks legally.

Scared

"Last Friday I was scared—my boss almost fired me!"

Shame, ashamed

It's a shame for you not to make good money—when others do it so easily.

Sick and tired

Sick and tired of a wet basement?

Stranded

Avoid getting stranded on the road to small business success.

Sucks, sucks big-time

Slow Internet sucks.

Suppose this happened

Suppose this happened on YOUR wedding day!

The _____ of your dreams

The 9-iron of your dreams.

Throw away

Throw away your specs!

Ugly

The ugly truth.

Unfortunately

Unfortunately, paying your business taxes is not optional.

What have you got to show?

After all these years of hard work and long hours, what have you got to show for it?

When I was, when I did, when I had

When I was 16, my father died of a heart attack.

Why does, why did

Why does every man hope his first child will be a boy?

Worry, worrying
Should you still worry about getting AIDS?

Stroke the Reader's Ego

You may have heard a cynical person tell you, "Flattery will get you nowhere." But more often than not, flattery will get you precisely what you want it to get you: to please and create goodwill with prospects.

One of the most powerful emotional tactics in persuasive and sales writing is to flatter the readers and stroke their egos. People like to feel important. And they like to be recognized as superior in some way. For instance, if you are writing to a list of vegans, praise them for having the wisdom to choose a healthier diet and the compassion to stop the cruelty of killing animals for food.

Or, if your target audience is affluent people to whom you are selling million-dollar homes, acknowledge the wealth they have accumulated and their success in career or business that helped them achieve it. Of course, do so without making those who inherited their money feel second-best; instead, talk about their family's legacy of success.

Appeal to customer ego by incorporating these words and phrases into your copy:

Accomplished
An accomplished woodworker deserves to be doing his craft on a Powermatic Lathe.

Best, the best, better
Are you one of the best at your trade? We think so!

Distinguished, distinguishes
Your company's safety record distinguishes yours as one of the top 1 percent plants for safe operation.

Exceptional

As an exceptional parent, you want to help your children be exceptional, too.

Favorite

A special gift for our favorite customers only.

Generous

Your generosity to our cause is about to be rewarded with a handsome tax credit.

Handsome, trim, fit, good-looking

Only a few of our customers are fit and trim enough to wear this sexy, stylish sports bra.

Hard-working, work hard, how hard you work

We know how hard you work. And a small token of our appreciation is enclosed.

Hero

You're it—the hero of American business!

Honest, honesty

A special announcement for salespeople who believe honesty is the best policy.

Important

You're important enough for us to extend this special invitation to become a platinum member.

Independent

A special invitation to the hero of the American insurance industry—YOU, the independent agent.

Knowledgeable, knowledge
Only a collector with extensive numismatic knowledge will thrill to the story of the 1874 Morgan silver dollar.

Leader, a leader
You're a leader in your field. We think we are in ours, too.

No-nonsense
You're the kind of no-nonsense small business owner with whom the Howard Bank loves to do business.

Original, an original
You're an original; there's no one out there quite like you.

Preferred
A special offer for our preferred customers only.

Recommended
Your peers have recommended you as an outstanding member of the medical community.

Rich, affluent
You have to be adventuresome and bold—and affluent—to join us for our next Alaskan cruise in June.

Self-sufficient, self-made
As a self-made millionaire, do you secretly look down on associates you know were born with a silver spoon in their mouth?

Smart
You're smart. I'm smart. Every Carnegie-Mellon computer science graduate is smart. Or you wouldn't have a C-M CS degree in the first place.

Special

Here's why we think you are special.

Successful, success

If you're successful, why hide it with false humility? Drive a Bentley and show the world what you've achieved.

Top, tops

Congratulations on being voted by New Jersey Monthly *as one of NJ's top 100 dentists.*

Marketing to Businesses

A key differentiator in marketing to businesses vs. consumers is this: *the business buyer wants to—and indeed has to—buy.* Most consumer advertising offers people products they might enjoy but don't really need. How many subscription promotions, for example, sell publications that the reader truly could not live without? If we subscribe, we do so for pleasure—not because the information offered is essential to our day-to-day activity.

But in business-to-business marketing, the situation is different. The business buyer wants to buy. Indeed, all business enterprises must routinely buy products and services that help them stay profitable, competitive, and successful. For instance, if you are the plant manager at a chemical company and your pump is no longer capable of handling the increased volume of liquids your plant now processes, you have to buy a new pump. It's not optional. The proof that in business many purchases are mandatory rather than made on impulse is the existence of the purchasing agent, whose sole function is to purchase things.

Also, a large percentage of products and services for business and industry exist to solve specific problems; identifying the problems helps engage the readers' attention and convince them this product may be what they have been looking for.

While the language below is effective in all copy, it has been proven effective in tailoring copy and selling products to businesses.

Alternative
The ideal alternative to conventional gears.

Announcing the solution
Announcing the emissions control solution you've been waiting for.

Availability
Netgear routers have the highest system availability of any router used in residential local area networks.

Best-in-class
Best-in-class cooling towers for power plants.

Capacity
Dust collector increases filtration capacity with two main cartridges.

Compliant
100% compliant with EPA regulations.

Cost, costing
Is your pump costing you more than it should?

Cut, reduce, save
Cut mixer maintenance costs as much as 60 percent.

Do you need?
Do you need more air reserve for safer control of off-the-road equipment?

Downtime—saving, reducing, or eliminating

Oakite Engineering Cleaning Program saves three days of downtime with one drum of cleanser.

End

End bag damage for good.

Energy, energy savings, energy cost

How to solve your emissions problems—at half the energy cost of a traditional venturi scrubber.

Engineering, engineered

Engineered to light-weight automobiles for more miles per gallon.

Environmentally friendly

Our environmentally friendly design reduces particulate emissions by 98%.

Everything you need

Everything you need for rapid prototyping.

Expert solutions

Expert solutions for troubleshooting process control systems.

Fast, fastest

The B-47 is our fastest bomber.

First, first and only

First indirect gas-fired storage water heater for industrial use.

Free

This free policy saves money for Allied Stores.

Get

Get new simplicity in liquid chromatography.

Guarantee, guarantees, guaranteed

Pimlo lifetime drain line guaranteed against corrosion and leakage.

Heavy duty

Heavy-duty beauty . . . nickel-chrome plating over steel.

High-grade

Off-grade cotton can produce high-grade yarn.

How

How Hercules helps protect your roof.

How to

How to choose an acoustical ceiling to help prevent room-to-room sound transmission problems.

Human

The human side of pension planning.

Ideal for

Ideal for mixing fluids of different viscosities.

Industrial-grade

Industrial-grade cleaning equipment and supplies keeps your plant clean to prevent product contamination.

Innovation

Innovations from the aerospace industry enable can-making machines to run better and faster.

Just the right tool for the job

Grainger has just the right tool for every job.

Machined

Machined for tighter tolerance and precision fabrication.

Maintenance-free

INTECH gears have lubricant sealed within the bearing, making them virtually maintenance-free.

Make, make your

Make your power source 25% more efficient.

Mistakes

The 5 most common mistakes in mainframe network monitoring and how to avoid each.

New, now

Now—a new dispersant that gives fuel oils superior water-shedding properties.

No moving parts

No moving parts to clog or wear out!

Patented

This patented clip and stud makes Lyon your best shelving investment.

Performance

Goodway® VAC-2 delivers reliable wet/dry industrial vacuum performance.

Positive

How to implement positive discipline strategies.

Powerful

Easy, powerful, and extremely reliable AC drive.

Problem, problems

A special V-Belt Engineering Service to help you cope with 7 drive problems.

Productivity, production

How Thomas Corporation boosted production 77%.

Profit, profits

For full profits . . . sell the full Westinghouse auto bulb line.

_____-proof

Explosion-proof motors for safety-critical applications.

Qulet, quietly

Cleans quickly and quietly!

Reliable, reliability

Easy, powerful, and extremely reliable AC drive.

Safe, safety

A safe alternative to sulfuric acid.

Save

Save weight and space with the world's thinnest push rods.

Smaꙅhed

He smashed the sound-in-water barrier.

Tests

Tests prove it: fiberglass daylighting panels with DuPont Lucite fight weather best.

The answer

The answer you've been looking for to prevent gas leaks.

Total cost of ownership
Minimal chemical consumption means lower total cost of ownership.

Turnkey
The benefits of working with a turnkey manufacturer.

Which?
Which cast-iron groove was made in just 42 seconds?

Zone, zoned
Zoned controls boost production by helping increase operator efficiency.

CHAPTER 2

Grab Attention

The headline or subject line is the first thing the reader sees when she receives your promotion. Therefore, it is the job of the headline to immediately grab the reader's attention. Other elements of your promotion can also work to gain attention, most notably color and graphics—and on the Internet, sound and video. But the headline continues to play a primary role in getting people to stop and look at your ad.

Estimates vary, but various sources report that the average consumer is bombarded by literally thousands of advertising messages daily. Whatever the real number, we know that the consumer today is both extremely pressed for time and overloaded with material to read, watch, and listen to. Therefore, the need for strong attention-getting headlines is greater today than at any time in the history of marketing. Here are some words and phrases that have proven their attention-getting powers through extensive real-world testing.

Note: You often hear people proclaim that today consumers have the attention span of a goldfish, which is eight seconds. If that were true, you could not cook a meal, play golf, read a novel, or do your work. It's a B.S.

statistic. But it is probably accurate to say that your *headline* or subject line has eight seconds or less to grab the reader's attention.

These are tried-and-true keywords and structures for effective headlines:

" " [Quotation marks]

"After Over Half a Million Miles in the Air Using AVBLEND, We've Had No Premature Camshaft Failures."

$ [Dollar amount here]

Link 8 PCs to Your Mainframe—Only $2,395.

[A vs. B]

How to Solve Your Emissions Problems—at Half the Energy Cost of Conventional Venturi Scrubbers.

[Active verb here]

Try Burning This Coupon.

Amazing

Amazing but true . . . this letter from London.

Announcing

Announcing a Painless Cut in Defense Spending.

Are you_____

Are you between the ages of 45 and 74?

As Crazy As It Sounds

As Crazy As It Sounds, Shares of This Tiny R&D Company, Selling for $2 Today, Could be Worth as Much as $100 in the Not-Too-Distant Future.

? [Ask a question in the headline]

What Do Japanese Managers Have That American Managers Sometimes Lack?

Available

Surgical Tables Rebuilt—Free Loaners Available.

Banned

This stem-cell arthritis treatment, banned in the USA, is legal and available in Panama.

Behind closed doors

What George Bush Was Told Behind Closed Doors.

But wait

But wait. There's more!

Buy

Buy Scott Towels.

Change

Your body changes 500+ times a day. Your deodorant should keep up.

Diary

The diary of a lonesome girl.

Did you know?

Did you know your PC is exposed to an average of 37 hacker attacks each week?

Discover

Discover the secret to outperforming the market!

Do you have_____on your mind?

Do you have home security on your mind?

Do you know?

Do you know how to quickly find a lawyer?

Do you recognize?

Do you recognize these 7 early warning signs of high blood pressure?

Don't forget

Don't forget Noma Lights.

Enjoy

Enjoy more Face Time.

_____est (i.e., loudest, fastest, biggest)

At 60 Miles an Hour, the Loudest Noise in This New Rolls-Royce Comes from the Electric Clock.

Fast, Faster, Fastest

Develop Software Applications Up to 6 Times Faster or Your Money Back.

Find

Find your new favorites—check out these new additions . . .

Foods you should_____

3 foods you should never eat.

Free

New FREE Special Report Reveals Little-Known Strategy Millionaires Use to Keep Wealth in Their Hands—and Out of Uncle Sam's.

Hate

Don't you hate driving in rush-hour traffic?

Hidden

Hidden Treasures of the Northeast.

Hoax

The great oil hoax: What George Bush Was Told Behind Closed Doors.

How, How to

How to Avoid the Biggest Mistake You Can Make in Building or Buying a Home.

How much?

How much is "worker tension" costing your company?

How often?

How often do you hear yourself saying: "No, I haven't watched it; I've been meaning to!"

Ideas, bright ideas

Ideas for a quick-service restaurant.

Imagine

Imagine Harry and me advertising our PEARS in Fortune!

Instant

Instant Incorporation While U-Wait.

Irresistible

Cookies so irresistible you'll want to spoon 'em.

Is this the end of _____?

Is This the End of . . . Overeating?

It's not what you think

The One Internet Stock You MUST Own Now. Hint: It's NOT What You Think!

Just like [Name person here]

Stay One Step Ahead of the Stock Market Just Like Martha Stewart—But Without Her Legal Liability!

Kind, its kind, this kind of

It's the only juicer of its kind.

Little-known / Under-publicized

Earn 500+% Gains With Little-Known "Trader's Secret Weapon."

Master

Master the skill of network administration.

Naked, buck naked

Do you like how you look standing in front of a mirror when you are naked?

Next

Next Stop: Adventure!

Now

The 5 Tech Stocks You Must Own NOW.

Now you can

Now You Can Create a Breakthrough Marketing Plan within the Next 30 Days . . . for FREE!

Now you can get

Now You Can Get $2,177 Worth of Expensive Stock Market Newsletters for the Incredibly Low Price of Just $69!

One thing

I did this one thing and was set for life!

Par

5 reasons why your lawn isn't up to par.

Questions to ask

7 Questions to Ask Before You Hire a Collection Agency . . . And One Good Answer to Each.

Rewards

Rewards await bold speculators who want big returns this year.

Save/savings

Act now and save $10 off the list price.

Secrets, secret weapon

Unlock Wall Street's Secret Logic.

Sex, sexual

71-year-old man has sexual congress 5 times a day.

Should you worry about _____?

Should you worry about getting AIDS?

Straight Talk

Some straight talk about wide-screen TVs.

Take

Take the Chevy challenge.

Test / Challenge

Will Your Scalp Stand the Fingernail Test?

The curse

The curse of too much money!

They

They Laughed When I Sat Down at the Piano . . . But When I Started to Play . . .

Tomorrow

They drove 5 years into tomorrow.

Unique/uniquely

Your legacy should be as unique as you are.

Unlock

Unlock Wall Street's Secret Logic.

What; what do?

What Do Japanese Managers Have That American Managers Sometimes Lack?

What if

What if you timed your stock trades with the FIFA World Cups?

Why

Why Most Small Businesses Fail—and What You Can Do About It.

Why on Earth?

Why on Earth would you buy a new car without all-wheel drive?

YOU:

YOU: a confident public speaker!

You can now

You Can Now Subscribe to the Best New Books—Just as You Do to a Magazine.

You must / You should

The Retirement Investment You Must Make NOW.

You're never too old

You're Never Too Old to Hear Better.

Announce Something New

People are naturally interested in what is new. It arouses both curiosity and excitement. When you have a new product to advertise—or even a new version of an old product—trumpet this newness in your ad copy. It will increase readership and stimulate response—grabbing attention, creating an emotional engagement, and accomplishing many of the goals presented in these pages. Announcing something new is versatile and effective; do it by including this language in your copy:

Breakthrough

New breakthrough from Harvard Medical School gets rid of painful shingles fast!

Discovery, discover

NASA discovery for growing food in space now helps reduce arthritis pain and swelling.

First, first time, first time ever

Now for the first time ever—a sump pump that keeps your basement dry even when the power goes out!

Innovation

A major innovation in prosthetic limbs.

Just published

Just published—The Dictionary of Insurance Terms.

Latest, the latest

The latest upgrade to the HP LaserJet line of printers.

New, new and improved

New "Polarized Oil" Magnetically Adheres to Wear Parts in Machine Tools, Making Them Last Up to 6 Times Longer.

News

Have you heard the latest news about Cisco routers?

Recently discovered, recent development, recent

Recent development prevents computer thieves from stealing data stored on old computers you dispose of for recycling.

Spotlight

Restaurant Spotlight—find the right spot for any craving or occasion.

What's new?

What's new in portable insulin pumps?

Highlighting First-to-Market Status

If you are marketing a new product and there's nothing else like it, you can say you have "the first and only." Once competitors begin knocking off your design or idea, and making look-alike versions of your original design, then you just say "the first" or "the first and still the original." Consumers see companies that are the first to bring a new product or technology to the marketplace as innovators, which makes the business's star rise in the public's eyes.

In addition, many buyers, both business and consumer, are excited by and highly value innovative products and innovative companies. So if you are the first to bring a new market, it is axiomatic that you are the innovator in that product category—and saying so gets customers interested, even excited.

Signal your first-to-market status with words like:

Announcing
Announcing a new way to prevent cold bathroom and kitchen floors.

First, first and only
Introducing the first and only Caribbean Cruise as good as its brochure.

Never, Never before
Never before has Valley Bank offered this $50,000 in overdraft protection.

New innovation
A new innovation in truck rear lift-gates.

NB. "New innovation" is deliberately redundant to put extra emphasis on the innovative nature of the product or offer.

Not available in stores
The new Craftmatic® Adjustable Bed is sold only direct from the manufacturer to you. It is not available in stores.

Nothing else, nothing else like it
The new high-resolution Samsung touch-screen tablet. There's nothing else like it.

The only one, the only, the one and only, the only one of its kind
Now Acme is the only supermarket offering prepared vegan dinners—right in the produce section.

Unique
A unique new way to lower your health insurance rates.

Unorthodox
Suddenly multiply your income with unorthodox strategies like these.

We thought of it first
Tires that won't give you a flat even when you run over a nail . . . . And we thought of it first!

Emphasize Innovation

"First to market" makes you an innovator. But it is not the only way to innovate. You can innovate many parts of your business other than by inventing a new product. For instance, you can innovate with:

- A better warranty or guarantee.
- Offering financing, installment payments, or leasing.
- Using a different pricing model.
- Extended service contracts.
- New accessories.
- New sizes.
- New colors.
- New packaging.
- A new design.
- A new material.
- And many more.

Bring attention to this novelty with language like:

_____2.0
Get ready for telemedicine 2.0 with instant and remote physician access to your test results, totally HIPAA-compliant.

A fresh approach
Why not try a fresh approach to search engine optimization?

A new concept

A new concept in housing: building low-cost dwellings from metal shipping containers.

A new idea

Here's a new idea for cutting your electric bill up to 25% a month.

A new twist

A new twist on an old favorite: sugar-free apple pie à la mode.

A radical change, a radical departure

Electric cars running on rechargeable lithium-ion batteries represents a radical departure from the first electric cars built in the 1800s.

Change is in the air

Change is in the air at Dustco Bag Filters.

Cutting edge, leading edge

We're on the leading edge of treating arthritis with stem-cell therapy.

Forget _____

Forget what you've heard—France is affordable!

Impact

The Impact of Voice-Activated AI on Business Today.

Is no longer

Sales is no longer a boys' club.

Latest discovery

Experience the latest discovery in home energy-efficiency improvement.

Reshape, reshaping

4 trends reshaping health insurance.

Shortcut

Is there a retirement shortcut savings?

State of the art

3D printers are the state-of-the-art in rapid prototyping, though benchtop mills are giving them stiff competition.

The first, the first and only, the world's first

At last, the first sugar-free yogurt that actually tastes good!

The next generation

The next generation of laser eye surgery is finally here.

We wrote the book on, from the folks who wrote the book on

Commercial banking from the folks who wrote the book on electronic data interchange.

Give the Reader News

As a teenager, Thomas Edison earned extra cash for his experiments by hawking newspapers on the streets and in the subways. He noticed that if nothing special was going on that day, sales were slow. But if there was a major news event, the paper sold out quickly. People are interested in news!

News gets attention. People want to know what's new, similar to the way they are drawn to innovation. In print and online, stories that give news get much higher readership than ads that are pure sales pitches. For instance, email messages that talk about a major event happening that day get more clicks than timeless and evergreen emails. Add a news element and your readership, and response rates will improve. Here are the words and phrases to do it with:

A new dimension

Brings a whole new dimension to the spa experience.

Booming

The marijuana business is booming in the U.S.

Breakthrough, revolutionary, discovery

Johns Hopkins breakthrough helps asthma sufferers breathe easier.

First ever, first of its kind

The first electric lawn mower that mulches as it cuts.

Have you heard, have you heard about?

Have you heard the good news about wind energy?

Important

The most important discovery for straightening crooked teeth since metal braces.

Important news

Important news for women with thinning hair.

Incomparable _____

Incomparable reliability—goes 500 miles on a single charge.

Introducing the first

Interesting the first electric nose hair clipper that actually works!

Latest

Shop the latest arrivals by size.

Never before seen

Never before seen—a genetically altered tropical fish for your aquarium that glows under blue light.

New and improved
The new and improved lightweight tent for campers and hikers.

New hope
New hope for children who have trouble keeping up in school.

New idea
A new idea for supplementing Medicare.

New twist
A new twist on an old favorite.

New way, new approach
A new way to keep your hedges evenly trimmed—without a hedge clipper.

Newly discovered
An "organic fertilizer" that feeds your gut bacteria and keeps them healthy.

One-of-a-kind
A one-of-a-kind chocolate shake that curbs hunger and takes the weight off.

Opens up
Opens up new possibilities for hang-gliding and sky-diving enthusiasts.

Pioneer
Dr. Adams is a pioneer in the new robotic surgery.

Revolutionary
A revolutionary approach to helping dyslexic children read.

Something is happening, something just happened
Something incredible is happening to this pot stock.

Step ahead

A step ahead of other invisible dog fences.

Unique

A unique approach to do-it-yourself drywall.

Unlike any other

Unlike any other room heater you have ever used.

What's new

What's new in wearable technology!

Years ahead of our competitors

A programmable microwave oven years ahead of our competitors.

You may not be aware

You may not be aware that there's a simple way to get preventative health screenings.

You won't believe_____

You won't believe how sensitive our baby monitor is—lets you hear everything!

You won't believe your eyes

So compact and easy to store, you won't believe your eyes.

You'll wonder

So effective yet simple, you'll wonder why no one ever thought of this before.

You're never too old

You're never too old to hear better.

Convey a Sense of Urgency

Conveying a sense of urgency in your writing has two benefits for you. First, the orders come in faster, improving your cash flow. Second, and more important, urgency increases the total *number* of orders.

Reason: Experience shows that *a decision deferred is a decision not made.* Therefore, you want your prospects to respond immediately. If they put your ad or email aside for later consideration, they will likely never get to it, and you won't generate a lead or order. Therefore, one of the writer's tasks is to get readers to act now instead of later—and you can encourage that action with this language:

Act now!

Act now to claim your free gift!

After that, it's too late; before it's too late.

This offer expires Friday at midnight. After that, it's too late.

Be the first

Be the first on your block to protect your home with an ESSC alarm system.

Before

Before You Buy: A Guide for Choosing a Customer Data Platform.

BOGOF (buy one, get one free)

Buy 1 get 1 free.

But I urge you to hurry

But I urge you to hurry. This special offer is for a limited time only, and once it expires, it may never be repeated again.

Deadline

The deadline to take advantage of this special offer is Friday at midnight.

Deadline fast approaching
The deadline to get your free GPS is fast approaching. Don't miss out. Order now.

Die
"I had one foot in the grave. My doctor sent me to the nursing home to die."

Don't delay
Don't delay. Order cable today and get all major sports channels free!

Don't miss
Don't miss these shopping events.

Door will slam shut
The door will slam shut again right at midnight on Wednesday, May 28 . . .

During_____
Four ways to invest during bear markets and recessions.

Ends, ends tonight, ends today, ends this week
Spring Equinox Sale ends tonight with limited-edition sets at specially marked prices.

Final days
These are the final days for Huffman Furniture's going-out-of-business sales.

FREE gifts, gift
FREE Gifts Enclosed!

Get an early start
Get an early start and have a greener, lusher lawn this summer.

Get the latest

Get the latest driveway sealant—now available.

Give me X days

Give me 5 days, and I can give you a magnetic personality . . . let me prove it—free.

Hit the road

Hit the road with new coverage and thousands of miles.

Hop to it!

Hot to it! Our bunny chocolate lollipops are the perfect Easter treat.

If not now, when?

A new career could be yours. But YOU have to take the first step. If not now, when?

Instant

Instant relaxation. Lower your stress in 4 short weeks.

Isn't it about time?

Isn't it about time to ensure your family's financial future?

It takes only

It takes only 15 minutes a night to set yourself up to make a fortune.

It's time; now is the time; maybe it's time

It's time to fight back against high property taxes.

Just in time

You're just in time to test-drive the new Mazda CX-5.

Last chance

This is your last chance to own this handsome volume for only $9.95.

Limited time, time-limited

This special offer is for a limited time only, and once it expires, it may never be repeated again.

Madness

Shrub Madness: Save up to 40% on select shrubs and trees.

Major development

A major development in shingles prevention.

Next ____ Days

How to make an extra 5K to 20K in the next 30 days.

No more

Only so many copies of the premiere issue will be printed—no more.

No time

No time for Yale—took college online.

Now, now more than ever, now is the time, right now

Order now and we'll eliminate the 4th payment.

Offer expires March 21, 2020

But I urge you to hurry. This offer expires March 21, 2020, at midnight. After that, it's too late.

Out of time

You're almost out of time to collect your 50% savings.

Preview

Preview the new Jeep Cherokee—just in at our dealership this week.

Quicker

The quicker you visit our showroom, the more likely we are to still have some of the new models still in stock. But, they are going fast.

Release, released

Just released—Chicago's Greatest Hits.

Right away

Get your free rate quote right away and see how much you'll save.

SALE! This weekend only!

To celebrate the holiday, we are having a store-wide sale this Saturday and Sunday.

Say "yes" today

Don't delay—say "yes" today!

Send for it

Send for it today risk-free.

So little time

So many deals, so little time.

Soon enough

Caught soon enough early tooth decay can actually be repaired by Colgate.

So what are you waiting for?

This offer will soon expire. So what are you waiting for?

Start today, start right away, start now

Start now and earn $1,000 within the next 60 days.

Still need a _____?

Still need a Valentine's Day gift?

There's still time
There's still time for Valentine's Day delivery.

These savings won't last.
These savings won't last, so why not pay less now rather have it cost you more later on?

This may be your last chance
This may be your last chance to make a killing in gold.

This year
Reduce your build heating and cooling costs by 50% this year.

Time is running out
Time is running out to sign up for WorkTango's upcoming webinar, "The Evolution of Employee Voice."

Time limited, limited time
This offer is for a limited time only.

Today
Today—add $25,000 to your estate for the price of a pair of shoes.

Tonight
Tonight at midnight, we hand over our Tennessee Electric properties and a $2.8 million tax bill.

Too late
Is it ever too late to pursue a dream?

What are you waiting for? What's holding you back?
Rooms and suites at our resort are nearly booked full for the summer. What are you waiting for?

What will you do?

What will you do when your personal assets are seized to satisfy a judgment against your corporation?

You must act now

To reserve your tickets, you must act now.

Enhance the Deal

Giving the consumer something extra—typically something she was not expecting—helps merchants close more sales.

Good copy can make the reader desire your product, yet in some cases, she will not be convinced by your sales message and will not order. In sales lingo, she is not yet able to "pull the trigger"—take the final action and click or call—for a variety of reasons. Perhaps she is concerned about cost . . . or doesn't buy from companies and brands she doesn't already know . . . or is worried that installing and learning to use the product will be too complicated or too much work . . . or read a negative review online . . . or any of dozens of other factors that make her hesitant to take action, despite her interest and desire.

So here's how enhancing the deal solves this problem: if your sales copy has already sold her on the product, but she is sitting on the fence or thinking it over, throwing in one more extra option, item, or benefit, often at the last minute, can often make her decide in your favor. When someone is sitting on the fence, it can often take only a small push to get them over to your side.

The enhancement you add to your offer is called a "deal sweetener." In Yiddish, it is known as the *glicken*. The deal enhancement may not be a vital part of your product. But it can often produce a huge increase in your conversion rates and sales.

Create urgency by enhancing the deal, and use these phrases to do so:

Accessories included
Order today, and all attachments and accessories are included at no extra cost.

Batteries included
The remote control runs on two AA batteries included with your order.

BOGOF
Buy one pair of glasses at America's Best and get a second pair free!

But here's an even better deal
But see my P.S. below for an even better deal!

But wait. There's more.
But wait. There's even more at Schaumer Cadillac waiting for you . . .

Free Bonus
Click the button below now to claim your FREE Bonus Gift!

Free shipping and handling
Orders over $50 and get free shipping and handling.

It's the icing on the cake
Yes, free in-home service is the icing on the cake—but sometimes, the icing is the best part of the cake!

Just for you
A special birthday discount just for you.

Mystery gift
Order by midnight, and we'll send you a valuable extra—a "mystery" gift we know you'll enjoy.

Save

Save $10 on your next order—just use the discount certificate enclosed.

Surprise, surprise gift, special surprise

There's one more thing you get when you join AAA today—a surprise I know you'll love.

Take a closer look

Take a closer look and see what else is waiting for you inside.

Who else

Who else gives you free floor mats when you buy or lease a car?

Yours FREE

This special St. Jude's medallion is yours FREE when you order your leather-bound Gideon Bible now.

Date Motivators

A "date motivator" is simply a reason or incentive to respond, click, read, order, or take another action by a specific date. Here is a summary of the basic categories of date motivators in order of effectiveness:

- *Specify the date*—give the exact calendar date by which the reader must respond to take advantage of the offer, and even better, give the time, too; usually in online promotions, we say midnight.
- *Number of days to respond*—for instance, telling prospects they must reply within XX days to take advantage of the offer.
- Specify the time range of period—e.g., Easter, Christmas, "this year."

- *First come, first served*—without actually saying whether the offer or the supplies are limited in any way, "first come, first served" motivates the prospect to faster action.
- *Time-limited offer*—tell the prospects that there is a time limit on the offer without specifying the closing date or the number of days left to act.

And here is how you present them:

After that, you'll pay more
These savings are for a limited time only. Once this sale is over, you'll pay more.

Date
The expiration date is fast approaching. Act now and don't lose out.

Deadline
But I urge you to hurry. The deadline to get this free gift is midnight this Friday.

Easter
Easter Essentials—Cutco brings families back to the table—shop now.

Extended
Cyberspring Sale Extended One More Day!

First come, first served
Orders are filled on a first come, first served basis.

Going fast!
These deals are going fast!

Hurry.
I urge you to hurry while inventory is still in stock.

In as little as

Be ready to work in as little as 4 months in doctors' offices, hospitals, and clinics.

It's time

It's time to get your hands dirty when dealing with data analytics.

Last chance

Last chance to save—ends tonight! Shop now and save up to $160!

Limited inventory

We only a limited inventory of this book in stock. Once they're gone, no more will be printed.

Make your move.

Make your move to Pleasant Ridge now—only 3 townhomes left.

Only _____ left

Only 11 days left to get in on the Charter Subscriber discount.

Order by, order no later than

You must order by October 15. After that, it's too late.

Spring Break

Spring break event—sale starts today.

The clock is ticking

The clock is ticking on these special offers.

Time-limited, limited-time

This offer is for a limited time only. And once it expires, it may never be repeated again.

Waiting, is waiting, waiting for you
Your new iPhone is waiting.

Win, win a
Win a year of Godiva—sign in and shop now!

Be an Early Adopter

"Early adopters" are people who feel they must own the latest and greatest new products and technologies as soon as they become available. By comparison, a "laggard" or "late adopter" will not be an early buyer of a new anything, whether a new smartphone or a new make and model of automobile.

Laggards are conservative consumers; they want to buy products that have been proven and have withstood the test of time. Early adopters are often motivated to purchase precisely because the product *is* new. The desire to own the latest and newest often overshadows considerations of price, value, or need. In most cases, you do not *need* to have the next generation of earbuds—you want to have them because they *are* new. Early adopters like toys and bright shiny objects! Encouraging early adopters to buy typically drives more sales than targeting laggards.

Make it clear that your product is that shiny object by using phrases like:

Be the first on the block
Your neighbors will turn their heads when you're the first on your block to drive the new Mini-Cooper—a breakthrough in compact car design and engineering.

Early bird gets the worm.
Of course, you could wait until all your competitors are running on our new 5G network—but it's the early bird that gets the worm . . .

Get in on

It's not too late to get in on the ground floor of the tiny software start-up some are predicting will be the next Microsoft.

Green with envy

Your garage addition will turn your neighbors green with envy.

Leader of the pack

With new energy and strength, you'll be the leader of the pack.

Next big thing

It's the next big think in driverless cars.

This is your first look.

This is your first look at the year's most relevant advanced embedded systems.

Turn your _____ green with envy

When your neighbor sees you cutting your grass with the new John Deere Riding Mower, he will turn green with envy.

Who else

Who else has a weed trimmer like this?

Warnings and Alert

Try this experiment. When you are talking or walking with another person, suddenly and unexpectedly shout the word "STOP!" And almost every time, they will stop whatever they were doing immediately. Why? Because in childhood we are conditioned by our parents to obey warnings, e.g., "Don't touch the stove," "Don't play with that tool." We are punished if we do not obey the warning, and so gradually, we become trained to obey warnings on command.

It continues this way throughout life. White-and-red traffic signs say

STOP, and if we ignore them, we may be in a serious car accident. We don't cross yellow banners that say CAUTION when we are walking near a construction site. You get the idea.

For this reason, warnings and alerts are effective tools in persuasive writing because *they immediately grab the reader's attention.* Some psychologists, trainers, and others call this a "pattern interrupt." When you break the natural rhythm or tone of a piece of writing with a sudden STOP or other sudden warning, it gets the reader to wake up and pay more attention.

Break natural rhythm and get a reaction with these words:

Burst
How the cobalt price bubble just burst!

Danger
2 big dangers now facing every upper-income American . . . and one new investment strategy that can protect you against both.

Dangerous
Cleaner replaces dangerous solvents.

Disaster
New cash law will be a disaster for savers.

Don't
Don't throw away this letter!

Don't be fooled
America, don't be fooled: Donald Trump doesn't know what he's doing.

Don't go
Don't go to strangers when you are looking for a job.

Don't let

Don't let athlete's foot "lay you up."

Hidden dangers, danger

The hidden dangers of nut allergies at the holidays.

Illusion, just an illusion

That healthy garden is just an illusion.

In no uncertain terms

Michelle Obama explains in no uncertain terms why she won't run for office.

Killing, might be killing, may kill

Your pillow might be killing your neck.

No one is expecting

The massive stock market rally that no one is expecting.

On the verge

A pipeline project on the verge of failure.

On the way

A freezing cold winter is on the way.

Plague

The Plague of the Black Debt.

Read this before _____

Read this before you take the statin drug your doctor told you to.

Red Alert

Red Alert: Ukraine at risk of Russian attack ordered by Putin.

Shocking

Three shocking events that may wipe out millions of investors.

Signs, sign

One critical warning sign proves gold is in a bear market.

Starving, starving to death

Your garden is starving.

Stay one step ahead

Stay one step ahead of the stock market just like Martha Stewart—but without her legal liability.

Syndrome

The 4 syndromes of passivity in the face of pending tyranny.

The one food you should never eat

The one food you should never eat if you want to avoid type 2 diabetes.

Warning

Warning: Your Physician's Desk Reference is obsolete!

What you need to know

What you need to know before you agree to get an X-ray or CAT scan.

Unusual, Out of the Ordinary

Life can be exciting and challenging, but also at times ordinary and dull. People are naturally interested in the special, the odd, the unusual, and the extraordinary. Example: whenever a rare two-headed snake is found in the woods, the story invariable ends up in the local newspaper and online. Not only are people interested in things other than the ordinary as curiosities; they oftentimes like to own, display, and show off such items to friends and relatives.

You can leverage this psychology by presenting your product as unusual, and therein capture the audience's attention. This language will help you do it:

Adventure
Follow me on my strange adventure in day trading that made me a millionaire.

Arrogant
How An Arrogant Teen Drove Me over the Edge.

Banned
Once banned by the Canadian government, now 100% legal.

Change of pace
Pipe smokers—for a change of pace, try our new, smoother Red Cherry Tobacco.

Conversation starter
The Franklin Mint Civil War Chess Set is a real conversation starter when proudly displayed on your living room or family room coffee table or end table.

Crazy
Medical doctors can now help save dialysis patients with an artificial kidney, as crazy at that sounds.

Exotic
Not one person in a thousand has ever tasted this exotic spice.

Explore
Explore the possibilities of an exciting career as a medical coding specialist.

Hard-to-get

Hard-to-get comic books from the 60s and 70s now at Joker's Child.

Hell, like hell, hellish

Behind the Mueller Distraction . . . a Hellish Catastrophe.

In a class by itself

Our new multivitamin is in a class by itself. Here's why . . .

Insane

An insane credit card offering 0% interest until 2020.

New experience

Here's a new experience: a handyman who finishes the job on time.

New twist

Introducing a new twist on an old favorite.

Odd, oddity, oddest

Here's the oddest creature you can buy at a pet store—looks like a miniature flying saucer with a tail.

Offbeat, off the beaten path

Paradise Cove is off the beaten path.

One-of-a-kind

One-of-a-kind . . . is that phrase a little trite?

Rare

A rare opportunity to fly over the Hudson River . . . in a hot air balloon!

Remarkable

The Glock G41 handgun fires with remarkable accuracy.

Unusual, unusually

Unusual "inversion" in the precious metals markets may double your investment within 6 months.

_____ with a difference.

Now experience family health care with a difference.

CHAPTER 3

Create a Perception of Superior Value

A primary objective of marketing copy is to create or enhance the perceived value of a product. The reason for doing so is as follows: if you can convince the prospect that the price you are asking for your product is a drop in the bucket compared with the value it delivers, you will have an easier time making the sale. Therefore, the greater the perception of value, the more orders you will get.

One of your jobs if you have a role in marketing is to help formulate, support, and evolve your company's "value proposition"—a statement that, in just a few sentences, clearly and concisely communicates how your company delivers value to customers in excess of the fees or prices you charge for your services or products.

The Unique Selling Proposition (USP) is one of the more powerful ways to frame your value proposition. The USP (see Appendix IV) clearly defines the most important benefits you provide along with how you are different and better than competitors in your niche.

Consumers see value in a wide range of product attributes including quality, durability, design, functionality, reliability, speed, and brand. When you link these attributes with your product's features and benefits, you help create a perception of value in the reader's mind. Here are words and phrases that can help highlight the virtues and value of your product:

$_____

$25,000 whole life insurance.

Add

Add 25 yards to your drive.

Award-winning

The award-winning new fragrance by Michael Jordan.

Awesome _____

The new Impressionist wing at the Modern Museum of Art is nothing short of awesome.

Bargain

Money-saving bargains from America's oldest diamond discount house.

Best-in-class

The Westinghouse TPS-43 is a best-in-class airport radar system.

Best-of-breed

The Westinghouse TPS-43 is a best-of-breed airport radar system.

> **NB.** "Best of breed" is simply a variation of "best in class." It too unambiguously states that the product is superior to any and all of its competitors. Use this phrase mainly when writing to *Fortune* 500 and executive types, because it smacks of business-speak a bit.

Beautiful

Healthy, thick, and beautiful hair

Bespoke

Isn't it time you treated yourself to a bespoke suit?

Better and faster

How to Write Better and Faster.

Beyond the dreams of avarice

Mastering entrepreneurship can make you rich beyond the dreams of avarice.

Bigger

Everyone needs do so something bigger than life at least once in their lifetime.

By storm.

The keto diet craze is taking the country by storm.

Certified, certificate of authenticity

Each commemorative coin comes with a certificate of authenticity.

Charming

Charming embroidery and fluid fabrics.

Classic, classics, the classics

Classic rock from the 80s—now available on CD.

Could this be?

Could this be the most powerful weight loss program ever devised?

> **NB.** "Could this be" lets you imply that your product is #1 in its category, but in a question format that makes the claim seem less like outright boasting.

Custom, customized

A 5-blade, hydrating, customizable power tool that also shaves.

Decadent

Freshly dipped perfection: luscious strawberries meet rich, decadent Godiva chocolate.

Delicious

Frosted Lucky Charms; they're absolutely delicious.

Deluxe

The New Monarch Super Deluxe—a Great Bike!

Distinctive

A distinctive lifestyle deserves a distinctive real estate experience.

Dreams, dream

The swimming pool of your dreams for less than you imagine.

Durability

Rugged construction delivers superior durability.

Elegant/elegance

The enduring elegance of a black pearl-and-diamond bracelet.

Endurance

Ford trucks are first in endurance.

Engineered

Carefully engineered hydro-massage jets sooth tired muscles.

Enriched

Pillsbury's now enriched with two important B vitamins and iron!

Environment, good for the environment

Our hybrid uses 50% less gas on highways and even loss on open roads, helping the environment with few emissions.

Essential, essentials

Garden essentials: turn chores into pleasures with quality tools and accessories.

Experience_____

Experience an unparalleled smoke with this fine whisky-infused cigar.

Experienced

No one is more experienced than Wagner Auto.

Fine _____

Fine linens—at YOUR price!

Five-star

For five-star results, shouldn't you call a plumber who has five-star reviews online?

Free

It's yours free. Won't cost you a penny.

> **NB.** "Free" is also one of the most powerful words in the English language. Giving the consumer a free gift or bonus adds to the value of her purchase. When something is free, say it many times so the prospect is 100 percent clear that there is no cost. Example: "The first issue is free. There's no cost of any kind. You pay us nothing."

Genuine

Genuine Steerhide Huaraches: the sandals that made Mexico famous.

Gold mine

Greatest gold mine of easy "things-to-make" ever crammed into one book.

Greatest, great

The Greatest Shredder in the World.

Guarantee, Guaranteed.
Your satisfaction is 100% guaranteed or your money back.

Handcrafted, handmade, etc.
Handwoven by the mountain people of New Mexico.

Head and shoulders
The Dodge Viper stands head and shoulders above any other car in its class.

Heirloom
A beautiful heirloom carpet you will keep for generations.

Impeccable
Come dine at a 5-star French restaurant with impeccable service.

Important
The most important day in America in 50 years.

Innovation, innovative
An innovative approach to making smart clothing with built-in wireless devices.

Instrument
The instrument of the immortals.

Investment-quality
These are investment-quality coins in mint condition.

It's the Rolls-Royce of _____
It's the Rolls-Royce of color printers.

> **NB.** You can create an instant picture of value in the reader's mind by comparing your product to a premium product in another

category—in this case, Rolls-Royce. The readers instantly visualize a Rolls-Royce and then associate it with your product in their minds.

Largest, large
New Jersey's largest selection of metal and stone outdoor fire pits.

Like no other
An umbrella like no other.

Magical, magic, magically, like magic
A magical and revolutionary product at an unbelievable price.

Miracle
Miracle glasses—I knew the glasses worked, but I didn't realize their new power.

Much sought-after
1950s Chevrolets are much sought-after by classic car collectors.

None better
Our personal trainers are tops. There are none better in the county!

Not one person in 1,000 has _____
Not one person in 1,000 has tasted these Royal Riviera Pears.

> **NB.** The phrase "Not one person in 1,000" connotes rarity and exclusivity—two factors that raise a product's perceived value.

Once difficult, now easy
Piloting a high-powered speed boat—once difficult, now easy.

Only _____ made, only _____ left in stock
Only 100 made. Grab these exclusive styles while supplies last.

Only, one and only

New Jersey's Only Comprehensive Cancer Center.

Perfect, perfection

Freshly dipped perfection: luscious strawberries meet rich, decadent Godiva chocolate.

Performance, outperforms

Outperforms models that cost thousands more.

Power, powered

Don't buy any low-priced car until you've driven the new Plymouth with floating power.

Premium

Try our rich, premium-roast coffee.

Priceless

Priceless protection for finer foods.

Proven performance

Our all-wheel drive has proven performance on ice and snow that 4-wheel drive cannot match.

Pure

Pure comfort—easy-wear styles.

Reasons why, reason

7 reasons why TV commercial directors prefer Unilux strobe lighting.

Reliability, most reliable

Reliability unmatched by any other car in its price range.

NB. Prospects want to know the reasons why your product is superior. "Reasons why" serves as an introduction to a clearly delineated list of product advantages, usually presented as numbered points, which is easier for you to write and for the prospect to read.

Safe, safety features, built for safety, safest
The Humvee, built like a tank using military engineering, is one of the safest vehicles you can own.

Reward, rewarded
Get rewarded just for being an AT&T wireless customer.

Right out of the box
Dress shoes feel great right out of the box.

State-of-the-art
The Chevrolet Volt is powered by a state-of-the-art lithium-ion battery.

Strongest
The strongest fabric every devised for boys' clothing—guaranteed.

Super, superior
Super all-wheel control.

Supreme
Las Vegas's supreme entertainment venue.

There's no better value
There's no better value than a GE refrigerator.

There's no comparison
There's no comparison between window air conditioners and central AC.

Top-of-the-line
Top-of-the-line installation and service.

Ultimate
The ultimate desktop organizer.

Unduplicated, unmatched
Our quality and craftsmanship are unduplicated in the industry.

Welcome addition
A welcome addition for your coin collection.

While you sleep
Lose weight while you sleep.

White-glove service
Our crew prides itself on delivering white-glove service.

> **NB.** The term originated when servants wore white gloves so they could easily tell if there was dust by running a gloved finger over the surface.

Who else wants?
Who else wants to make $250,000 a year as an independent marketing consultant?

Without compare, beyond compare
The new impressionist wing at the Modern Museum of Art is beyond compare.

Without question or quibble.
If you are not fully satisfied, your money will be promptly refunded—without question or quibble.

World's finest
Introducing the world's finest artisan blue cheese.

Worth, worthy
Practically worth its weight in gold!

Wonderful
Down from Canada come tales of a wonderful beverage.

You
YOU: a successful small business owner.

> **NB.** "You" is one of the most powerful words in the English language. Readers don't care about anything more strongly than themselves. Prospects perceive added value in a product that speaks directly to them and their needs.

You'll be a hero
When you implement the AS/400 in your data center, you'll be a hero in your IT department.

Stand-alone Value Keywords

"Stand-alone" value keywords convey your value proposition on their own, with no comparison to other solutions. The classic is Sugar Frosted Flakes: "They're GREAT!" It doesn't say how the cereal is better than other cereals. It doesn't compare Frosted Flakes with other breakfast options. It simply says, "They're great!" On the face of it, seemingly not terribly specific or powerful. But "Sugar Frosted Flakes—They're Great!" has endured for decades.

Affordable
There just isn't a more affordable tub on the market.

Amazing, amazingly
We use an amazingly resilient fabric that got top marks during our rigorous lab testing.

Beneficial
Taking this probiotic may have beneficial effects on your digestion.

Better
Feel better.

Critical
Becoming proficient in Excel is critical to getting hired for almost all white-collar jobs today.

Favorite
Commonly known as peony, these flowers are an old-fashioned favorite whose bloom can grow up to 10 inches across—and they can live to be 100 years old!

Improve, improved
Improve your communications with a new AT&T phone.

Indispensable
Precision Reeds—indispensable to serious clarinet and saxophone players.

Insulated
FREE insulated travel bag.

Look, a look, the look
Get the Look with Medieval Collectibles.

Luxurious, luxury, luxuriate
Relax and luxuriate in a hot bath in a Kohler tub after your workouts.

Perfect
The perfect mood for your favorite moment.

Practically
This mat is so smart, it practically does yoga for you.

_____proof

Corrosion-proof vinyl gutters never rust, erode, or develop pinhole leaks.

Reward yourself

Reward yourself with a pedi-mani at Beaumont Nail Salon.

Security

Job security working in the healthcare industry.

Significant

Significant relief from your aches and pains.

That's where _____ comes in

That's where ESC's insulated cabling comes in.

Top

Top 4 interior design projects that can boost home value.

Treasure, treasures

Mediterranean Treasures. Rarely Seen.

Win, winning

5 ways speakers can win back distracted audiences.

Associative Value Keywords

"Associative keywords" associate the product with something else of value. For instance, an ad for a face cream declared it was like a "face lift in a bottle"—implying it got results as good as plastic surgery, but at a tiny fraction of the cost. The cereal Wheaties uses the slogan "the breakfast of champions" to associate the product with the nutrition regimen of top athletes.

Many of these set up similes, but more direct options are also possible:

As

Royal Riviera pears are as sweet as sugar.

As good as gold

Investing in silver—as good as gold—in fact, higher potential gain than gold at a fraction of the cost per ounce.

Award-winning

Our spirit of innovation drives award-winning technology.

Built like a tank

The Ford Silverado is built like a tank.

Can make you

How behavioral data can make you the Uber of the business-to-business world.

Closest thing to

Driving the new Corvette is the next best thing to being a NASCAR professional.

Greatest thing since

Wellington Scones are the greatest thing to come to the American breakfast table since sliced bread.

In a can, in a bottle

Liquid Plumber—the "plumber in a bottle."

Inspired by _____

Summer's favorite shoe comes in beautifully embroidered variations inspired by nature!

Like a _____

Recruit like a project manager.

Comparative Value Keywords

"Comparative keywords" create a favorable comparison between your product and others either in its field or used for the same application. For instance, Wonder Bread claimed its product superior to white bread, because only Wonder Bread "built strong bodies 12 ways." No other bread on the market made a similar claim.

Create winning comparisons for your product with this language:

Are better than

3 store-bought cake mixes that are better than homemade.

Before-and-after

Before-and-after photos show how DynaFlex builds rock-solid abs in just four weeks!

Best

You've tried the rest; now try the best.

Better

Better than barefoot: water shoes that protect in and out of the water.

Blows away

Henderson Chevrolet just blows the competition away!

Exclusive

Access to exclusive products.

Indispensable

Indispensable advice for men and women who want to quit work someday.

Leaves the competition in the dust

The Orek vacuum's suction is so powerful, it leaves the competition—but not YOU—in the dust.

Makes _____ look like _____

Grapes so large and luscious they make the store-bought kind look like birdseed.

MBA

Crash-course in business strategy is like getting your MBA in 8 weeks!

Never again

Never take a loss again with this strategy.

No other

No other crossbow even comes close.

Refreshing, refreshed

Stay asleep all night—wake up refreshed!

The one-and-only

The one-and-only Fast Track Costa Rica Conference.

World's greatest, world's best, world's most valuable

The world's greatest manual and most valuable course.

Adjectives and Phrases for Quality

I include this short section on words and phrases that bespeak quality with some hesitation. On the one hand, you, your client, or your boss may find many occasions where you want to emphasize quality without overusing the word quality.

On the other hand, saying you have a quality product or service is not as persuasive or potent as you may think, for two reasons.

First, it's a vague term. Nonspecific. Not descriptive. Not quantitative. Exposes you to consumer skepticism. And superior quality is a claim that will not be taken as face value: for consumers to believe the claim, you have to prove it, not just say it.

Second, quality is so overused that it has lost most of its meaning, power, and impact. It's a superlative, not a specific. The word quality has minimal attention-getting and credibility-building power in the marketplace of the 21st century.

Absolutely brilliant
Absolutely brilliant crystal that makes all others look like cheap glass.

Beautiful
Beautiful bulb gardens.

Better than store-bought
Curcumin Plus has twice the potency of store-bought turmeric powder.

Craftsmanship, impeccable craftsmanship
Made by skilled furniture workers with the finest craftsmanship.

Engineered
Engineered with the precision of a fine Swiss watch.

Genuine
Grundite Pavers are the genuine article!

Handcrafted
Handcrafted artisan cheese for the discerning palate.

Head and shoulders above the rest
Womack Wedding Planners stands head and shoulders above the rest.

Keeps its _____

A Slendersuit™ keeps its shape while it shapes you.

Lasts longer

Lycra® Xtra Life resists chlorine so your suit lasts longer.

Leader

The global leader in high-speed data communication.

Made in America

WeatherTech floor mats are made 100% right here in America.

Precise, precision

Precision engineered for maximum performance.

Show-stopping

Everything you need to grow show-stopping roses!

Sparkling

Sparkling charms guaranteed to dazzle.

Special

Cutco's Saturday Specials.

Standout

Hebrew National Hot Dogs: a standout at any backyard barbecue.

Surpass, surpasses

NetGear routers far surpass Optimum in reliability, versatility, and performance.

Ultimate

The ultimate in home gym equipment.

Vibrant

A vibrant residential community for seniors.

Adjectives for Attractive Appearance

We live in a world that considers beauty and appearance to be important attributes. You may find this superficial, especially when applied to human beings. Yet many consumers judge potential product purchases on appearance first, as if one *could* judge a book by its cover. Emphasize the aesthetics of your product with adjectives like these:

Beautiful, beauty, a real beauty

A beautiful set of uncirculated state quarters in a handsome wooden collector's display case.

Dazzling

Lady Gaga's outfit for the Super Bowl halftime show was absolutely dazzling.

Exquisite

These Fabergé egg replicas are exquisite in their design and faithfulness to the originals.

Flat, thin, trim, lean

The easiest way to a flat belly.

Flawless

Revlon gives you a flawless complexion.

Gorgeous

A gorgeous hand-painted porcelain collectible.

Handsome

A handsome bespoke suit for the man who has never owned perfect-fitting clothing before—now at off-the-rack prices.

Lean, trim, flat

The key to a lean, sexy stomach, toned legs, and defined arms.

Pretty

Pretty fresh flowers to grace your Thanksgiving table.

Spotlight

Spotlight on style: polka dots are back!

Streamlined design

The sleek, streamlined design makes BMW the ultimate driving machine.

Stunning

She'll look absolutely stunning in these quarter-carat diamond earrings.

Stylish

Stylish through any storm: Cute, classic, and water-resistant.

Quantity as Value

There is tremendous value to consumers in merchants who stock large quantities and offer wider selections.

For instance, if you are shopping for shoes, a small local mom-and-pop store has limited space, limited room for inventory, and limited selection—in brands, styles, colors, and sizes.

On the other hand, Macy's in NYC had, last time I was there, an entire floor—seemingly the size of a football field—devoted to shoes. So the selection was huge.

E-commerce sites, among other advantages like convenience of shopping and home delivery, also offer value to consumers in the quantity and variety of merchandise they sell. The proof is Amazon, which in 2018 generated gross product sales of almost $142 billion; they sell more than

606 million different products in the U.S. alone.[3] The enormous variety and number of different products adds tremendous value to online shoppers.

Follow this lead and highlight quantity in your copy.

[Number] [Product]

75 courses under $60—ends midnight tonight.

Giant warehouse, huge showroom, giant store

Our giant showroom has more pianos to choose from then any other store in the tristate area.

More

More chiropractors on staff than any other clinic in the state.

No other

No NYC camera store has a bigger variety of cameras, accessories, and supplies than B&H Photo.

Over

Over 30 fragrant roses—shop the sale now.

So many

So many dressed—20% off—5 days only.

The most

You'll find the most guitars on sale at Victor's House of Music.

Wide selection, widest selection

The Fair Lawn Russian deli has the widest selection of Russian and Ukrainian take-out dishes in Bergen County.

---

3   https://www.scrapehero.com/how-many-products-does-amazon-sell-worldwide-october-2017/

Cost Benefits

"Cost-benefit," also called in the business world cost-benefit analysis, is typically a superior metric for making purchase decisions vs. cost alone. If you buy on price, you often save the most money but also get the least value or the worst-quality product.

"Cost-benefit" means comparing two products based on the ratio of the benefit or value they deliver as compared to their cost. At the risk of oversimplifying, let's compare two models of Wi-Fi networks that can be installed in your home for better and more reliable Wi-Fi. The first is Google Wi-Fi and costs around $400. It will greatly improve wireless Internet reliability. But your computer guy tells you another option is Brand X Wi-Fi. It is supposedly a high-end system and even more reliable than Google Wi-Fi—but it costs $4,500.

You are doing this for your house, not your company, and $4,500 is a lot of money. So your cost-benefit analysis would have to balance the tenfold savings of Google's solution with the value to you of reducing wireless Internet access downtime to the absolute minimum, which includes the cost to you of being without wireless Internet access—a big problem if you run a business from home.

This is especially important if your product is high-end or is in a class of products that are generally more expensive. Encourage consumers to think beyond sticker price and highlight your product's superior cost-benefit with language like:

Beware of imitations, beware of imitations
Beware of imitations.

Challenge
Take the Pepsi challenge.

Compare head-to-head
Compare your beer with Guinness head-to-head—and see why yours doesn't stand up to ours!

Costs more but

Chivas Regal may cost a bit more. But it's worth every golden sip.

Don't settle

Don't settle for an SEO firm if it isn't top-ranked by Google for the key word SEO!

In its class, in its category

17 reasons why the Pelorus is the best yacht in its class among those costing $100 million and up.

Low cost, lowest cost

You'll get big-car quality at lowest cost.

No other, nothing else

Only Filterflo Oxygenators keep your expensive saltwater fish in your biggest aquariums vibrant and healthy. No other filtration system even comes close.

Pound for pound

Pound for pound, nothing delivers more power and protection on the road than a Humvee—except possibly a tank.

Sets the standard

Pall sets the standard by which all other tower internals are judged.

We've reinvented

Cessna has reinvented a way for you to fly your own airplane.

You'll pay a little more

You'll pay a little more for a Mont Blanc writing instrument. Here's why you'll be glad you did.

Stress Savings and Selection

Earlier in the book, we discussed how consumers value both a wide selection of products and reasonable prices. The jackpot for many buyers is the two together—"savings *and* selection"—a huge selection at great savings. This is what has made Walmart, Target, Alibaba, and Amazon the success stories they are today.

Keywords like the following will signal both for your prospective customers:

A few cents a day
Famous Five-Foot Shelf of Books Now Yours for a Few Cents a Day.

All
We carry all major brands at discount prices.

Alternative
A great alternative to overpriced wines.

An unbelievable price
A revolutionary product at an unbelievable price.

Assortment
An enormous assortment of semiprecious stones.

Broad range
A broad range of styles, sizes, and materials.

Cheap
Get thousands of gifts dirt-cheap—or even free!

Choose
Choose from many distinct styles and colors.

Clear choice
Chantrix is the clear choice when you want help quitting smoking.

Cut
Cut annual energy costs with Robertson Q-Air Floor System.

Dazzling array
Our greenhouses have a dazzling array of exotic cacti and succulents.

Deal
An incredible deal every day through June 28.

Extensive
An extensive selection of wedding and engagement rings.

Half price
Special half-price get-acquainted offer for a hard-to-believe introductory $32.45.

If we don't have it, we can get it for you.
At Briar Rose Books, if you don't see the book you want, ask us, and chances are we can get it for you.

Less Costly
Rich Man's Burial Now Less Costly Than a Simple Grave.

Pay too much, paying too much
You're probably going to pay too much in personal income tax this year.

Perfectly legal, 100% legal
137 Perfectly Legal Ways to Get a Check Out of Uncle Sam.

Rebate

You could pay all your closing costs with our commission rebate check.

Red tag

Red tag clearance sale on hundreds of items—up to 50% off PLUS free shipping!

Savings, Saving

Summer Savings Countdown!

Slash

How to slash the cost of your mortgage loan by 57%—with NO closing costs!

Special introductory price

That the seller has a lower price to introduce a new product adds a degree of credibility and a reason for the discount.

Spring sale

Over 200 plants up to 40% off.

Starting at

Hundreds of sofas to choose from, starting at just $229.95.

This _____ will cost you $_____

This book will cost you $19.50. Now here's why your good sense compels you to read it.

Thousands to choose from

We have thousands of motivational items to choose from, from posters and plaques to trophies and motivational posters.

Unrivaled selection

An unrivaled selection of wedding and engagement rings.

Wide selection

They're not just a steakhouse. They have a wide selection including seafood and pasta.

Win

Win a new Ford!

Would you risk?

Would you risk 83 cents a day to enjoy good health—guaranteed or your money back?

Zero

If you are not 100% satisfied, our home study course costs you zero. Zilch. Nada. Nothing.

Extend a Special Offer

In marketing parlance, an offer is simply what the customer gets when he responds to your promotion combined with what he has to do to get it, e.g., "Click the button below now for your FREE Special Report, 'How to Flatten Your Belly in Just 10 Minutes a Day.'"

To extend a "special offer" means to make an offer beyond your usual or ordinary offering. In the above paragraph, the product being sold was a weight loss supplement—thirty pills, a month's supply, per bottle at a retail price of $97 per bottle. The manufacturer extended the offer with three special components: First, buy eight bottles instead of one bottle now and pay just $24.95 a bottle. Second, an unconditional one-year money-back guarantee, enabling the buyer to get a full refund, without returning bottles, any time within twelve months of the date of purchase. Third, the free bonus report on how to flatten your belly.

Almost everything

25% off on almost everything.

At a price that may surprise you

Drive a certified preowned Infinity today, at a price that may surprise you!

Below cost, at our cost

Own this rare 1932 George Washington quarter for less than our cost.

BOGOF; two for the price of one

Buy one, get one free.

But see _____ for an even better deal

But see my PS below for an even better deal.

But wait. There's more . . .

Buy 2 shirts today and get a third shirt free. But wait. There's more . . .

Buy now, pay later

Buy new carpet for any room now on installment and make no payments until next year.

Call today

Call today for a FREE Cruise Guide.

Certificate

After taking our program, you get a handsome Certificate of Completion, suitable for framing.

Charter

Become a Charter Subscriber today and save!

Clearance sale

Valentine's Day Clearance Sale.

Closed

Closed to new investors for the last years—now open again . . .

Club

Thinning hair? The Hair Club for Men can help!

Coupon

20% coupon for 4th of July!

Courtesy transportation

Courtesy transportation provided for Premiere Members only.

Door is open again

The door is open again . . . and it just got easier than ever to "make money while you sleep."

Early-bird special

Renew your subscription today and save $25 with our early-bird special discount.

Enroll now

Enroll now to activate your membership benefits immediately.

Everything must go!

We're closing our store—everything must go!

Examination copy

Send for an examination copy to use at home for 30 days risk-free.

Exclusively

Made exclusively for you.

Free catalog

Call now for our free catalog.

Free consultation

Call today for a free consultation and review of your retirement portfolio.

Free delivery and installation

Free home delivery and installation included when you buy a 62-inch Samsung TV—this week only.

Free demonstration, free demo

Call Acme Filtration now for a free demonstration.

Free dinner

Retirement workshop—free dinner provided!

For members only

This life insurance is available to our members only.

Free estimate

Call Acme Siding now for free estimate.

Free needs assessment

You get a free needs assessments with a registered investment advisor without cost or obligation.

Free samples

Stop by the food court for free samples of our wings.

Free shipping

Free shipping on your next order!

Free training

Buy this new drone now and get a free 2-hour day training session at our store.

Free trial, free use

Take the Hedge-O-Matic hedge clipper for a free 30-day in-home trial.

Get

How to get thousands of FREE GIFTS.

Gift

20 unique gift ideas sure to please your daughter-in-law.

Half price

All winter coats are now half price.

Join

One-in-50 Americans can score high enough on an IQ test to join Mensa.

Kids are free, kids ride free, kids eat free

On Friday nights, kids eat for free.

Last chance

Last chance to get these fine diamond earrings.

Love

The season of love sales.

Lowest prices

If a competitor is selling this item for less, bring proof, and we'll match it.

May I?

May I send you 3 FREE Issues of what may be the most influential (as well as the most selectively distributed) newsweekly in the world?

Membership

Subscribe to Smithsonian *magazine and become a member of the Smithsonian today.*

No cost

There's no cost or commitment of any kind.

No interest, pay no interest, interest-free

No interest charges for 30 days.

No obligation

Send for our free DVD today. No obligation, of course.

Not available in stores

This special online offer is not available in stores.

Offer ends today

An effective call to urgency.

OTO—one time only

This is a one-time-only offer. Once you leave this page, you can never access it again.

Product refund

If you are not 100% satisfied, return the unused pills, or even the empty bottles, for a prompt product refund.

Quick-response bonus

Order within eleven days, and you get an extra bottle as a quick-response bonus.

Rebate

Get a $1,000 cash-back rebate.

Risk free

Try it for 30 days risk free!

Season, seasonal

Bring in Spring! Fresh Fashions! New Colors! Great Savings! 20% off your order + FREE shipping on orders of $25 or more.

Select

20-40% off select roses. Save now.

Send for it ... FREE

NB. "Free" is one of the most powerful words in advertising, and "send for it" prompts the reader to take action.

Send no money now

Send no money now. We will bill you later.

Sign-up bonus

New customers save 20% on first purchase with our sign-up bonus.

Sneak preview

Model homes—sneak preview.

Special anniversary Offer

Take advantage of our 25th anniversary sale. It's our anniversary. But YOU get the gift!

Special offer

Special offer for AARP members.

Surprise

Order now and get a surprise free gift worth $25!

This week, this weekend, this month

30 Must-Have Roses SHIP FREE This Weekend Only.

Today only

Freaky Friday sale . . . today only . . . $20 off + Free Shipping on Orders of $99+.

Volume discount

Buy a set of 5 collectible Star Wars glasses and get a 10% volume discount.

We're slashing our prices!

We're slashing our prices . . . . Crazy Eddy's prices are INSANE!

You win, you may have already won, you have won

You may have already won $5,000 a week in cash for life!

Yours

Yours exclusively—this beautiful Mother's Day charm bracelet.

Cost Reduction

One way to extend a special offer is through a "cost reduction," which simply means the price on the item has been reduced, either permanently or for a special sale. Or there is a special offer (e.g., Buy one, get one free). In cost reduction offers, the consumer saves money while the merchant lowers the price, either to sell more of the item or get more people to come into the store.

The biggest cost reductions are for "loss leaders." The loss leader is a product typically sold at or below cost. Because it's so favorably priced, it brings in a lot of orders and sales traffic. Prospects who place a phone or online order are immediately upsold to higher-priced items. In retail, loss leader offers can increase store traffic, and people who come into the store to buy the loss leader often end up buying much more—making the loss leader a profitable tactic.

A fraction of the cost, a small fraction of the cost

Our system delivers superior performance at a fraction of the cost of other brands.

Affordable, afford

Owning a John Deere has never been more affordable.

As low as

Monthly rates as low as $3.49 for adults.

At our cost

Own these uncirculated Silver Eagles—at our cost!

Buy __, get __

Buy 3 and get the 4th FREE.

Clearance, clearance sale

Save up to 70% on all sale and clearance styles.

Flash sale

FLASH SALE: Today and tomorrow only.

Fraction

A fraction of the cost of professional treatments.

Half price, half the price

All the PDF software you'll never need . . . for half the price. You get 50% off list price!

Hot, hot deals

What's hot on UPtv?

Never increase

Rates are locked in and will never increase for any reason.

Weekend deals

Weekend deals—save $10!

Ease of Purchase

Ease of purchase means what it sounds like: the merchant makes it quick and easy to purchase the item. Reducing obstacles to purchase is a great way to hook potential customers; use approaches like:

$_____ down

Now own Florida land—$10 down and $10 a month.

All credit cards accepted

We accept cash, all major credit cards, PayPal, and bank wire transfers.

Easy payments

Yours for just 3 easy payments of only $19.95 each.

Extended hours

Black Friday extended hours let you shop for bargains all day and all night long.

Just mail

Just mail back the order form today in the reply envelope enclosed. It's already addressed. And the postage is paid.

No money down

No money down, and your first payment isn't due until January 1st.

Send no money

Send no money now. We will bill you later.

Shop

Shop the sale now.

Simply call

Simply call us toll-free at 800-XXX-XXXX now. Operators are standing by.

Visit

Click on the link and visit our website now to order online.

Value Multiplier

A wealthy and famous 20th-century businessman, whose name I cannot recall, said, "It is not enough to give your customers their money's worth. You must give them *more* than their money's worth—more than they have any right to expect." The "value multiplier" is an offer that does just that: give them more than they bargained for. The multiplier may be multiple price savings (discount off retail price, another discount for rapid response, free shipping) or multiple benefits (a raincoat that keeps you dry and is comfortable to wear) or multiple features (free moon roof, free heated seats, and free Sirius radio). Salespeople and advertisers will often use these keywords to present their chosen multiplier:

An added bonus

As an added bonus, your state quarter collection comes with a free velvet-lined display case.

Case

Purchase eyeglasses today and get a free soft or hard carrying case.

Complement

Perennials that perfectly complement your roses.

Free [consumable supply]

Your rental car comes with a full tank of gas. And you don't have to refill it—you can even return the car with an empty tank!

Get a second _____ FREE

Buy one Swiffer today, and you get a second Swiffer absolutely free.

Just the start

Dry is just the start. Sure, it's totally waterproof. But this raincoat feels great, too. Thanks to the stretch.

Reduced Customer Risk

Reducing customer risk in a purchase is another form of a special offer. "Risk reversal" is a powerful marketing technique and sales closer.

In many transactions, such as buying a used TV at a garage sale, the buyer takes all the risk, because once you purchase an item at a garage sale or flea market, it's yours—there are no returns.

Risk reversal means taking some or all of the risk off the customer's shoulders and placing it on the merchant's shoulders, where it should be.

Strategies like the following will reduce customer risk but increase chance of conversion:

Ironclad guarantee, unconditional guarantee

You are fully protected by our unconditional money-back satisfaction guarantee.

Promise

If there is ever a problem with your order, we promise to make it right— whatever it takes!

Refund

Free refund if you are not 100% satisfied and return the item within 30 days.

Replace

If your new air conditioner doesn't cool your room to a comfortable temperature, we'll come to your home and either repair or replace it free of charge.

Stand behind

At Fischer Motors, we stand behind every preowned Buick we sell.

Warranty

You are protected by a one-year manufacturer's warranty on all parts and labor.

We pay for any damage

Our movers treat your furniture and possessions with the utmost care not to damage them. But if there is so much a tiny rip, tear, or scratch during the move, we take it to our shop and repair it to like-new condition—at our cost.

Company Reputation

What does company reputation have to do with special offers? Simply this: an offer is only as good as the company that stands behind it. Therefore, whether you are a reputable local establishment or a trusted global brand, you can strengthen your offer by pointing out that it is backed by a business the consumers knows and trusts: yours.

Better deal

No one has better deals on leasing a new Lincoln than Brooklyn Lincoln Automotive.

Good

Like a Good Neighbor, State Farm is There.

Industry leader

Jayco is the industry leader in hardened steel.

Quality

At Ford, Quality is Job One.

Trust, you can trust

Hermann Appliance Repair. The name New Jersey homeowners have trusted for over 75 years.

We have your back

We have your back. In a Swim Tee®, you're always safe from sunburn 'til the sun sets.

You can be sure

You can be sure if it's Westinghouse.

Capabilities

"Capability" or "capabilities" refers to the functions of a product, the skill set of a service provider, or the capacity, resources, and deliverables an organization can provide. For instance, if you hire a website designer to do a site for your business, you can't assume she has the capabilities to do search engine optimization (SEO) or back-end integration with your database; you have to ask.

Usually having more capabilities than the competition is seen as a competitive advantage. But you can create the reverse perception that "less is more" by positioning your product or service as a specialty. Example: companies that do SEO only are perceived by many potential clients as necessarily being more expert and competent in search engine optimization than vendors, such as website designers and digital marketing agencies, who do multiple digital marketing tasks and do not specialize in SEO.

Create a perception of comprehensive capabilities or of specialty with these key phrases:

A to Z

Everything you need for your garden from astilbes to zinnias.

Advice, advisory services

Advice to help you get your do-it-yourself project done . . . and done right.

Answer, answers, all the answers

You have questions. We have answers.

Comprehensive

Comprehensive kitchen design and remodeling services.

Consult, consultation.

A free initial consultation can point you in the right direction.

Design

We design it. We build it. We support it.

Everything, everything you need

Everything you need to become a successful day trader.

Fix

Our competitor gives $9 haircuts. We fix $9 haircuts!

Full range

We offer a full range of home repair services at prices you can afford.

High-capacity

High-capacity backup generator can keep all your lights and appliances on during a blackout.

Integration, system integration

Full system integration service means all your needs are handled by one single, reliable vendor.

Made simple, makes things simple

Austin Aviation makes planning your air travel simple.

Professionals

THE professionals in reverse osmosis water purification systems.

Protects

Protects your computer against transient voltages and surges.

Proven, proven success, proven expertise

Proven success in optimizing coal-fired power plant performance.

Single source

Clean Venture is your single source for containing oil spills on the land, in your building, and in the water.

Solve, solution

We have the tools and experience to solve your most pressing home repair problems.

That's where we come in, that's where we can help

Electrical wiring in need of an upgrade? That's where we can help.

Total package

Investor Center gives you the total package, meeting all your trading, investment, retirement, and estate planning needs.

Total solution

Acme provides a total solution from start to finish.

Turnkey

Koch Process Systems offers turnkey services from pilot plant testing to full plant constructions, support, and operation.

We do the work, we do it all for you

We do all the work. So you don't have to.

CHAPTER 4

Underscore Product's Advantages and Benefits

Perhaps the most basic tactic of advertising that sells is to communicate product features, advantages, and benefits to potential buyers.

A feature is what a product is or has. An advantage is a feature your product has that the competition does not. A benefit is what the feature or advantage will do for the buyer, how it will help him come out ahead.

For instance, a feature of a watering can is that it has a spout. The advantage of a watering can we bought at the garden center is that it has an extralong spout that others do not. The advantage is that the water can reach plants in the back of your plot or garden patch without your actually having to step over and possibly on top of other plants to reach the spot you want to water.

Beyond creating the perception of value as discussed in the previous chapter, give the more detail- and analysis-oriented customer the whole picture by presenting what your product does, how it does it, why it's important, and why it's customer-friendly. General terms like these below are a good start; more targeted key words and phrases are broken down by method in the pages that follow.

Adjustable
The resistance can be adjusted to give you the level of workout that's right for you.

Benefits
The benefits of working with a turnkey manufacturer.

Best, better
Better handling on snow and ice.

Boost, boosted, booster, boosting
Medical blood circulation booster.

Build, builds
Builds cash value for your family's needs.

Choose, you choose
Choose your hours—any time of the day or night.

Comfort, comfortable
Special fabric makes our T-shirts the most comfortable you'll find anywhere.

Compact
Compact stacked washer/dryer can fit any space even in the smallest of apartments.

Convenient
No other air purifier is more convenient—just set it and forget it.

Cordless, no cords
Built-in rechargeable battery means no power cords to trip over.

Easy

Easy to buy.

Energy-saving, energy-efficient, energy-efficiency

The high energy-efficiency rating of our new subzero refrigerator helps lower your monthly energy bills.

Fast, fastest

The Osteon Juicer is the fastest way to make fresh juice to start your morning with healthful vitamins and energy.

Head start

Give your children a financial head start.

Helps, help, helping

Helping the world invest better.

Improve, improves, improved

Test-drive the new and improved 2020 Cadillacs today.

Life-changing

Life-changing medical device.

No

No classes to attend, no schedules to keep.

Portable

Portable hair dryer fits easily in your luggage when you travel.

Quiet, quietly

Runs quietly.

Reliable, reliability

The highly reliable ITT trivalve pump ensures minimum downtime.

Relieve, relief

Relieves aches and pains.

Rugged

Rugged construction makes these garden tools last for years.

Saves

Automatic operation with no operator saves you time and money in your plant.

Stops

Stops house siding from peeling, warping, or coming loose even in the hot sun or high winds.

Time, save time, reduce time, cut time

Cut your time to hire in half!

Work at home

Work at home—earn up to $39,000 a year and more.

You get

You get all this.

Identify the Applications

When you say that your product is ideal or well suited for use in a particular application, you are by implication saying your product performance is superior when it is used in that application. You are also saying it is designed to meet the specific requirements of the application the buyer intends to use it for.

All-purpose

All-purpose sealant keeps water from penetrating cracked foundations, roofs with missing shingles, leaky gutters, and anything else in your house or vehicle you want to seal and make watertight.

Charge, charges

Charge any device without access to a wall socket with this solar-powered charging kit.

Create, creates

Create a living carpet to cover empty patches and suppress weeds.

Early warning

Early warning system—double wall heat exchangers let you detect leaks before crosscontamination can occur.

For

For handling harsh corrosive chemicals.

For every

For every type of rum drink.

How do you know?

With 403 companies making pumps, how do you know when to call Blackmer?

More demanding

There's no application more demanding than a metropolitan area network.

Repair, repairs

Repairs tears in leather upholstery so you don't even know they are there.

Streamlining

Made for streamlining your storage.

This is for

This is for guitarists who don't want to put up with annoying amp feedback.

Your problems

The worse your corrosion problems, the more you need DuPont Teflon®.

Document Key Features

A key feature is one that is either more valuable, more important, more unusual, more special, or more beneficial than other product features. Typically, it is unique and delivers a major user benefit.

Make a list of all product features you can think of. Rate them 1 to 5 with 1 = relatively minor and unimportant to 5 = of great importance to consumers. Then rank all the features rated 5 in order of priority. The top #5 is the key feature. Use keywords like these to highlight it:

All-day

The underarm deodorant you can rely on for all-day odor protection.

All-in-one

All-In-One Low-Priced Caribbean Cruises!

Batteries included

The first full-house generator with backup battery included.

Burst

Yellow Tiger sports drink energizes you with a quick burst of incredible energy.

Childproof

Our sliding gate will childproof your stairs.

Corrosion-proof

Weber grills are guaranteed to be corrosion-proof for the 2-year warranty period.

Customized

The settings are customized by the installer just the way you want them.

Cuts

Gas Energy Inc. cuts heating and cooling costs up to 50%.

Deserve

You deserve a break today.

Double, doubling

The secret to doubling your income or more—every single week!

Easy to manage, easier to manage

New software makes your investment properties easier to manage.

End

End defrosting forever with a Frigidaire Frost-Proof Refrigerator.

Extralarge

Available in large and extralarge.

Fade, fading

Our siding won't fade under any condition.

Fits in the palm of your hand

So compact and portable, it fits in the palm of your hand.

For

For deep-clean, oil-free skin, Noxzema has the solution.

Fun, make it fun

Wherever you go, it's fun to play!

Get a _____

Get a Sexy Body in 4 Weeks Flat!

Get rid of, eliminate

Get rid of painful kidney stones—without surgery.

Gluten-free

Gluten-free bread for easier digestion.

Hard-to-find

A wide selection of hard-to-find art supplies for hobbyists and professionals.

High-capacity

High-capacity backup generator can keep all your lights and appliances on during a blackout.

Hollywood

A Hollywood smile in 3 days . . . or your money back.

Impressive

An impressive list of credentials.

Instant relief

Let me show you how hand reflexology can bring you instant relief from pain.

Laser-cut

Laser-cut design.

Last, last longer

Ford Trucks Last Longer!

Lightweight

The lightweight projector is easy to lift and carry.

Lush

Add lush, tropical blooms to your home and garden.

Luxuriant

Handcrafted from luxuriant materials.

Makes the most of a limited space

Compact washer/drier makes the most of the limited space in your apartment.

Marvelous

A marvelous way to see Europe.

Massive

A Colossal Flub Brings You This Massive $22.75 Book for a Mere $9.95!

Meticulous

Old-world artisans build your furniture with meticulous attention to detail.

Microwave-safe

Heat up your food right in the microwave-safe container.

More

More of everything you want with Mercury.

Never again, no more

Can't fall sleep? Never Again.

Never be, never been _____

Never been unable to haul a full load.

No moving parts

Why you should buy a mouse with no moving parts.

Optimal, optimize

Optimizing Your Office 365.

Paid you

67 reasons why it would have paid you to answer our ad a few months ago.

Painstaking attention to detail

Each crystal sculpture is made with painstaking attention to detail.

Personalized

Personalized with your name laser-engraved, which removes the outside coating so the letters match the color of the gold-plated barrel underneath.

Powerful

Only Firestone Ground Grip Tires give you powerful backbone in the traction zone.

Precision

The pump that puts precision into flow.

Profit, profitable

Profit from the wisdom of over 50 investment experts.

Quiet, quieter

Lower rolling friction results in quieter operation.

Redundant, redundancy

Redundant sensors ensure you are protected even if the primary sensor fails.

Roomy

Drivers with families appreciate the roomy interior.

Safety

It's designed for extra safety!

Slipping through your fingers
If the money you're making is slipping through your fingers, our tax-free municipal bonds can help you keep more of it.

Streamlined, streamline, streamlining
First streamlined car planned for lookers and riders.

Stylish
Our stylish and high-quality potting benches become your garden command center.

Thrill
Enjoy the thrill of going to the beach with your new six-pack abs!

Turn, turns
Turns $100 into $10,000 in 2 weeks.

Versatile
Splint-Lock is a simply beautiful, effective, and versatile chair-side splinting technique.

Who would have thought?
Who Would Have Thought I'd Make So Much Money Without Going to College?

Why ... ?
Why swelter through another hot summer?

Highlight Special Features

A special feature is a product attribute that most other products in the category do not have. For instance, when you install a chip in a product to give it added "intelligence," that's a feature today called "smart." For instance, there are smart refrigerators that tell you when you need to buy milk; smart cars that automatically brake if the vehicle in front of you stops suddenly and you don't respond quickly enough on your own; and smart homes that allow you to control them (e.g., turn on the lights remotely) via your mobile. And smart is just one example of a special feature; there are countless more.

Special features exist in virtually every product category. Services, too. For instance, my home's central air is serviced by the only company in our county that has round-the-clock technicians who are on call to come to your home 24 hours a day, 7 days a week—important in the summer when the AC stops working at noon on Sunday and the interior of our house slowly become a steam bath.

Absorbable
Highly absorbable Curcumin Plus is absorbed by your body 7 times better than turmeric powder.

Electric, electrical
Wallflower amplifies the effects of its room air fresheners by enhancing distribution of the droplets with an electrical dispenser.

Encapsulated
The probiotics are encapsulated with a protective coating to prevent the nutrients from being destroyed by harsh stomach acids.

Lightweight
The machine's lightweight components reduce noise and increase rolling speed.

Low-friction
Low-friction cylinders move easily and reduce power requirements.

Rechargeable
Special rechargeable lithium-ion batteries can last more than 5 years.

Self-cleaning

The new self-cleaning electric oven saves time and effort.

Self-lubricating

The self-lubricating crank shaft never needs oil.

Smart

A "smart processor" inside the sneaker tells you when your pulse or heart rate is too high while running.

Specially designed

The King 2166 3B valve trombone is especially designed for trumpet players who want trombone as a second instrument but don't want to learn to use the slide.

Wear, no wear, minimal wear, prevents wear, prevents wear and tear

Polarized oil magnetically sticks to metal cutting edges for superior lubrication that prevents wear to machine parts.

Underscore Product Advantages

When a product has an advantage over other brands in the same category, emphasize its advantage in your copy. Unique advantages especially should be pointed out, as should advantages that deliver important user benefits. Remember, consumers are constantly asking why one brand is better than all others in its category. Often a unique advantage others cannot provide is the answer. Pair this strategy with your "comparative keywords" from Chapter 3.

[Use non-rounded numbers]

Ivory Soap—99 44/100 percent pure.

> **NB.** When making a claim with numbers, you increase its attention-getting power and credibility by not rounding off, e.g.,

"Make $4,970" is stronger than "Make five thousand dollars" or "Make thousands of dollars."

Afford, affordable
Now you can afford the finest television with the highest resolution available in TV today.

And so much more
For fall L-band detection and so much more.

Beautiful, beauty
Beautiful polished blue topaz diamond and topaz pendant.

Best
Life's best moments . . . furnished.

> **NB.** Be careful when using "best." It's better to have someone else say it—a media source, expert, or customer—rather than you saying it about yourself. The former is more credible, and the latter sounds like boasting and creates skepticism. Also, without proof to back up the claim, competitors may challenge it.

Breeze, breezy
Designing is a breeze with new UltraGraft II CAD 2.0 Software.

Burns
"Negative calorie" foods burn fat while you eat them!

Comfortable, comfort
The comfortable all-day easy-stretch pants.

Convenient, convenience
Pop Tarts are a convenient, quick, delicious breakfast you can eat on the go!

Decrease, decreases

Crest toothpaste with fluoride decreases tooth decay.

Delicious

Salada is delicious iced tea—refreshing, too!

Dependability

Presidential Insurance—All Dependability.

Do you suffer from _____ ?

Do you suffer from bunions or heal spurs?

Economy

For long-term economy, specify Mueller Infrastructure for all modifications to your water mains.

Experience

Experience the vacation of a lifetime.

Extra

Extra pleasure, extra comfort, no extra fare.

Extra Cash

Extra Cash$$$$.

Extraordinary

Explore the origin of extraordinary.

Eye-catching

An eye-catching crisscross pattern is just one of many styles to mix and match.

Farm-fresh

Farm-fresh, from our fields to your table.

Finally

Finally, a simple smartphone anyone can use—even technophobes!

Fresh, Freshly

9 out of every 10 of my customers buy freshly ground A&P coffee.

Go ahead

Go ahead and eat the foods you love.

Good news

Good news for those with hearing loss.

Greatest

The greatest market discovery ever made.

High-Performance

For high-speed, high-performance data integration, look into Magic Mirror.

Impervious

Aluminum gutters are impervious to rust or corrosion.

Ingenious

37 Ingenious Spare-Time Businesses.

Legendary

Legendary customer service.

Less, lower, reduced

Sealed ball bearings require less maintenance.

Like new

Whitens dentures like new.

Live

Watch live games on your smart mobile with a Prime Video MBL.TV subscription.

Long-lasting, longer-lasting

Energizer Batteries are longer-lasting.

Love

Your dog shares the spirit of the wolf. And his love for meat.

Maximum, maximize

Nitric oxide maximizes blood flow through veins and arteries.

Miracle

Miracle glasses.

Money, make money

How you can make real money selling life insurance?

More

Paratherm provides more energy savings and greater heat transfer efficiency for thermal fluid system users.

Natural

100% natural—no artificial ingredients.

New, a new kind of

A new kind of freezer . . .

New and improved

New and improved Havoline motor oil.

No

No filter replacement required.

No one
No one colors your world like Le Vian.

Nothing else
Nothing else you could place on your walls is in such perfect taste, so sure a touch of refinement.

Of our age, of the century
The most important advance of the century in cardiac care.

Old-fashioned, old-fashion
Old-fashioned butter cookies, just like your mother used to make.

On steroids
Clean your siding in half the time with a power-wash system on steroids.

Onsite service
We offer onsite service so you don't have to lug your unit to the store or ship it back to the manufacturer, both of which are pains in the neck.

> **NB.** Customers who need repairs or service would rather you come to them than they come to you. Obviously, they'd like free onsite service, but if this convenience costs them a reasonable sum, they normally don't have a problem with it.

Optimal, optimum
Beta-sisterol supports optimal prostate health.

Original
The original sun-washed canvas.

Perfect, perfection
The hunt is over for the perfect cheesecake.

Power, powerful, high-powered
Superior power performance from heavy-duty industrial rectifiers.

_____-proof
Hole-proof, run-proof, rip-proof hosiery with reinforced nylon mesh.

Pure
Welch's for pure enjoyment.

Push-button
Revolutionary push-button ironing.

Radiant, radiantly
The radiantly soft tee shirt with yarn spun from the top 1 percent of the world's cotton.

Real
Real leaf-brewed tea.

Refreshes, refreshing
The pause that refreshes.

Remarkable
A remarkable value.

Reveal, reveals
Reveal the beauty within.

Robotics, robotic
Removing prostate cancer with robotic surgery.

See why
See why My Pillow gives you greater sleeping comfort!

Slice
Slice 20 years off your age.

Slimming, slim
Slimming but comfortable capris.

Smart
This mat is so smart it practically does yoga for you.

Solutions, solution
Creative solutions for timeless design.

Time-saving
Time-saving transportation and flagship hospitality.

Top
Own the flooring chosen by top designers and home builders.

Tough, tougher
New, tougher double-layer housing solves breakage problems.

Transforming
Transforming travel on America's waterways.

Trouble-free
Maytag appliances are trouble-free.

Unduplicated
Our system produces results unduplicated in the industry.

Unmatched
Our system produces results unmatched by any biometric access control technology.

We put it all together for you

At Hoopis, we put it all together for you.

When it comes to

When it comes to paying air travel claims, no one flies faster.

Winner

Winner of the J.D. Power Award.

Works for you

A broker who works for you, not for the seller.

Stress That Product Is Quick and Easy to Use

One of the primary advantages consumers and business professionals seek in products, services, and systems is that they are quick and easy to use. "Quick" because people are eager and impatient. "Easy" because people dislike complex and difficult tasks, and many of us are lazy and avoid hard work. These keywords are commonly used to convey both:

Easy, easier

Cheap and easy ways to stay in touch with tech.

Even a beginner, even a newbie, newbies

A home business so easy, even a beginner can do it!

Foolproof

Foolproof turf tip sheet helps you win at the track.

In no time, in no time flat

Put it together in no time flat—no tools required.

Instant
Just take it out of the box, plug it in, and enjoy instant warmth in the coldest room in your house.

It's a breeze
It's a breeze to learn Spanish with Rosetta Stone.

No sweat
Bad credit? No sweat at Murphy Ford.

Piece of cake
Makes passing the Post Office Exam a piece of cake.

Quick and easy
A quick and easy way to test your blood pressure at home.

Simple, simplified, so simple
Simplified operation makes it easy to trim hedges and bushes!

So easy
It's so easy, even a child could do it.

Snap
Installing the Toro irrigation system is a snap.

Step-by-step, simple steps, easy steps
Step-by-step instructions make installing your Toro underground sprinkler system a breeze.

Straightforward
Now learn a straightforward approach to getting new patients.

User-friendly
User-friendly desktop computer designed especially for the disabled.

Without headaches, without aggravation
Maintain a weed-free lawn without headaches or aggravation of any kind.

Stress Customer Service and Support

Customer service has always been a factor that significantly contributes to buyer satisfaction and business success. In today's digital world, users of high-tech products and services absolutely rely on technical support to keep their devices and appliances running. We are so dependent today on technology—everything from air conditioning and the refrigerator, to reliable electric power and heat, to Internet access and smartphones—that nothing irritates customers as quickly and severely as poor reliability, system failure, and downtime. So any copy that presents the customer-service benefits of your product has an advantage.

All day and all night
AAA is standing by to assist you on the road all day and all night.

At our expense
If you are not 100% satisfied with our work, we will redo it at our expense.

Available, available 24/7
You can reach one of our service reps—NOT an answering service—24/7.

Caring, care
Our customer service team knows that they have to care about your business, or you won't come back to ours.

Cater
We cater to your every need.

Confident, confidence
With a 98% positive customer rating, we're confident that we can fix your problem, too.

Dedicated

Our service department is dedicated to your total satisfaction.

Expert, knowledgeable

Our knowledgeable technicians have on average 25 years of experience.

Fix

If we don't fix it to your satisfaction, we'll come back and make it right—at our expense.

Flawless

Fiats are restored with flawless attention to detail.

Friendly

Friendly service reps answer your every question.

Genuine

Our service department only uses genuine GM parts straight from the factory and fully protected by the manufacturer's warranty.

Hands-on

Hands-on attention to every detail of the work.

If you will let us.

We can double the speed of your computer. If you will let us.

In stock

We have a large inventory of spare parts in stock, so we can make your repair without having to order the part from the factory.

No appointment needed

Bring in your smartphone for immediate service—no appointment needed.

No job is too big or too small.

NB. Allays a common customer fear: their job is too tiny for you to take on or too big for you to handle.

Our customers tell us
Our customers tell us our support is the best in the industry.

Phone call, only a phone call, just a phone call
Our service technicians are always just a phone call away.

Professional
Each professional IT consultant working on your system has a BS in software engineering or higher.

Respond, responsive, guaranteed response, quick response
Our support team is always responsive to your needs.

Round the clock
Service technicians are available to help you round the clock.

Serving
Serving the entire tristate area.

Text
Need service? Text us and tell us where you are and what the problem is.

We'll be there in a flash
When your car is stranded by the side of the road, AAA will be there in a flash.

We'll take care of the rest.
Furnace problem? Call us now. We'll take care of the rest.

Stress Convenience

Today's busy, time-pressured consumers place a huge value on convenience. Evidence of this is that there are now sixty thousand 7-11 stores in seventeen countries. More proof is that convenience stores can charge a price for a product that is 25 to 100 percent higher than what the consumer pays for the exact same product in the local supermarket. Buyers will pay a large premium for added convenience, giving convenience a strong sales appeal. Emphasize the convenience of your offering with these phrases and watch engagement increase:

A ____-minute drive
Just a 5-minute drive from the town square.

Adjustable, adjusts
Exercise bike adjusts resistance and incline to provide the level of workout you seek.

Armchair shopping
Fun and easy armchair shopping on QVC.

At your fingertips
Fresh fruit right at your fingertips.

Attach, attachment
Snap-on hose attaches in seconds.

Automatically, automatic
New aquarium heater maintains the ideal temperature for your tropical fish automatically; never needs adjustment.

Convenient
Convenient holders let you strap your water bottle to your bicycle frame.

Designed

Designed for indoor and outdoor use.

Easy peasy

Just snap on the nozzle and you're ready to go. Easy peasy!

Fits

Lightweight counter fits in the palm of your hand.

Floats

Ivory soap—it floats!

Ideal for _____

Ideal for left-handed golfers.

In minutes

Up and running in just minutes for instant humidity relief.

In the privacy of your own home, at home

Send for a risk-free Examination Copy of the first course lesson you can review in the privacy or your home or office.

Just _____

Just heat and serve in your oven or microwave, right in the tray. Ready in minutes!

Minutes away, in minutes

You can see a doctor within minutes of your arrival, even if you have no appointment.

Never needs _____

Filter never needs cleaning.

No more

No more waiting for a table with new drive-in pickup service.

On demand

Watch classic horror movies on demand.

One size fits all

Elastic pants belt—one size fits all!

One-stop shopping

One-stop shopping for all your DIY project materials, supplies, and tools.

Organized

Keeps medical records organized for fast retrieval when seeing new doctors or specialists.

Plug-and-play

Plug-and-play universal adapter enables portable electronic devices to run on the local electric current in any country in the world.

Portable

Portable battery charger for campers and others on the go.

Push button

Starting the Amana dishwasher is as easy as just popping in the soap pouch and then pushing a button!

Right around the block, around the corner, down the street

For your convenience, we've just opened a new branch that's practically around the corner from you.

Say good-bye to _____

Say good-bye to paper billing and check writing.

Self-_____

Motorized self-closing cover makes it quick and easy to close your swimming pool for the season.

Self-cleaning

Self-cleaning ovens eliminate one of the messiest household tasks.

Time-saving

A time-saving device no homeowner should be without.

Without hassle or headache

Get your driveway shoveled fast when it snows, without hassle or headache.

Stress Safety

Among the key motivators of human action is the desire for safety, security, and protection from harm. In Maslow's Hierarch of Needs, safety is identified as the second-most important need, right behind physiological needs such as food, shelter, and health. There are many products for the home, factory, and travel whose primary function is to provide safety and security for the user. Example include air bags, alarm systems, fire protection systems, baby monitors, smoke detectors, fences, gates, locks, road flares, and surveillance cameras.

Use these keywords if your product is one of those—or has any safety features you can use to assure potential customers:

Alert

Wearing a Medical Alert device keeps seniors safe by summoning quick help should they fall, get hurt, and be unable to get up.

Blocks

Blu-Blocker® sunglasses block the harmful blue spectrum of sunlight, which can cause the most damage to your retinas.

Compliance

Compliance with building codes keeps apartment buildings safe and sound.

Defense

A lightning rod is your first line of defense against damage from a thunderstorm.

Foil, foils

Specially designed wallet foils pickpockets from stealing your billfold, cash, credit cards, and ID.

Insulates

A comprehensive homeowner's policy insulates you from fraudulent claims of injury on your property or sidewalk.

Insures

Insures you against liability should you cause bodily harm to others in an auto accident, whether it's your fault or not.

Look at, looks out

Looks out for intruders 24/7.

Peace of mind

A home security system with central station monitoring gives you greater peace of mind.

Prevents

Cat litter is an effective stand-in for salt to protect you and your family from slipping on an icy sidewalk or driveway.

Protection

The Hartz collar protects your dog from fleas and ticks while eliminating itching and scratching.

Put your mind at ease

Install Yale door locks and put your mind at ease.

Safe, safety, safety-tested

Oversize bike reflectors keep you safe from careless drivers at night.

Secure

A $100,000 term life insurance policy from Mutual Assurance keeps your family financially secure should the worst happen to you.

Shields

SP-50 sunblock shields your skin from sunlight that can cause deadly melanomas.

Stop, stops

Mace can stop the most dangerous attacker in his tracks!

Take care

You just give our technician access to your electrical panel. We'll take care of the rest.

Why take chances?

The Taser Bolt is a quick and effective deterrent and defense against muggers. Carry it with you when you're away from your own neighborhood. Why take chances?

Stress Performance

The consumer expects the product to work exactly as advertised and prefers to purchase products that demonstrate proven and superior performance. Your product should perform as advertised, and your copy must convince the buyer that it does so repeatedly for hundreds or thousands of customers.

Adaptable

Adapts to a wide range of temperatures, winds, and terrains.

Automatic, automatically

Automatic tracking and email notification always let you know when your flowers have been delivered.

Boosts

Boosts the Wi-Fi signal in your home so wireless users are always connected.

Cuts

Cuts product contamination, metal wear, and skidding to a bare minimum.

Delivers

Delivers power and speed unmatched in the industry.

Does the job

When it comes to unclogging drains, pipes, sinks, and toilet, Liquid Plumber does the job.

Halts, stops, and even reverses

Prime Intelligence dietary supplement halts, stops, and even reverses loss of cognition and memory in men and women age 50 and older.

High-performance

The new Ford Mustang is the top high-performance driving machine in its price range.

Into your 60s, 70s, 80s, and beyond

Supports optimal joint health into your 60s, 70s, 80s, and beyond with this 100 percent natural remedy for replenishing synovial fluid.

Lowers, lower

Lowers your blood pressure to 125/85 or below without prescription drugs, surgery, or spending your life in the gym.

Maintains

Scotts Turf Builder® maintains a green, lush lawn you can be proud of all summer long.

Pays off

Insulating your walls and roof before the weather gets cold with Fomo Spray Foam is simple and quick and pays off in greater comfort and lower heating bills.

Quiet operation

A backup generator that runs so quietly, you won't even know it's on unless you look at the indicator panel.

Reduces

Reduces the appearance of wrinkles within 10 minutes of applying the cream to your face.

Reliable, reliability

Only FedEx has a reliability rating for on-time delivery for ground shipments of 98.7%.[4]

Surefire

A surefire way to make sure your basement stays dry with Fennimore French Drains.

---

4   https://www.supplychaindive.com/news/ups-usps-fedex-holiday-delivery-late
     -shipments/514862/

CHAPTER 5

Give Proof of Effectiveness

When you say your product is the fastest or most reliable, prospects are instantly skeptical, because everybody claims the same thing.

All product claims in marketing copy and content should be backed by proof. Here are some ways to convince wary buyers that what you say is in fact true:

1—Comparisons. Comparison—showing how your product is different from and better than others—engages the reader's attention. You can do a before-and-after comparison showing the change before and after the product was used, e.g., the dirty wastewater discharge vs. the clean water that has been treated with your filtration cartridge. You can also do a side-by-side comparison showing how your product outperforms the competition.

A very effective technique is to have a table listing all the features that your category of product could have. One column shows your product with a YES or checkmark indicating you have all the features. The other columns have competitor products with only a few checkmarks and the majority of spaces left blank or marked NO to indicate that they are lacking the feature.

2—Tests. An extremely compelling way to prove performance is to allow the customer to test your product, especially on their premises. For instance, a pelletizer is a machine that presses powdered material into pellets. The main question is how well the pelletizer will work with the customer's material. Mars Mineral solves this problem, telling potential buyers, "We'll be glad to take a look at a random 5 gallon sample of your material. We'll evaluate it and get back to you with our equipment recommendations. From there we can do an exploratory pelletizing test, a full day's test run, or rent you a production machine with an option to purchase."

3—Samples. Let the prospect sample your product. This is an old tactic. Eateries in shopping mall food courts often have a person standing in front of the counter with a tray of free samples of one of their dishes, whether egg rolls or chicken nuggets. Tempur-Pedic® offers a free kit in its commercials; the kit includes a sample of their mattress material. By squeezing and pressing it, you can prove to yourself their claim that the mattress material comfortably fits the contour of your body.

One company manufactures mist eliminators, which remove entrained liquids in gases exiting an industrial smoke stack. Their mist eliminator is a wire mesh that bends and twists much like a Slinky. In a direct mail campaign, the manufacturer mailed small samples of wire mesh to process engineers. The sales letter was printed on off-white card stock and affixed to the wire mesh so it looked like a shipping label.

4—Visualization. When prospects can see how something works, they are more inclined to believe that it does work. The mist eliminator company described above also made trays that enhanced efficiency in distillation towers. Part of what takes place is the liquid rising through capped holes in the tray and bubbling on its surface.

Normally, distillation towers are made from brick or metal, so you cannot see the trays operate. For their trade show booth, the company made a simple model of a distillation tower out of Plexiglas so process engineers visiting the booth could see the bubbling action.

Gore-Tex manufactures (among other things) a putty-like sealant that is used to prevent leakage in piping connections. The front cover of their sales brochure shows a picture of a pipe flange. Attached to the flange is an actual sample of the Gore-Tex sealant. Not only could prospects visualize how to apply it properly, but they could also remove it from the brochure to touch, feel, and play with.

5—*Dramatization.* Years ago, to promote sales of its disaster recovery systems and services, U.S. West mailed an audiocassette to telecommunications managers. When the recipient played the cassette, they heard the background noise of a busy telecom center. Then, suddenly, the CD went blank and the noise disappeared. A voice-over narrator said, "This is the sound of a telecommunications disaster waiting to happen." They dramatized the danger in a meaningful way without actually cutting off the prospect's telecom system.

6—*Description.* A manufacturer of digital switches for wireless networks wanted to convince telecom managers that their switch was highly reliable. Here is what they wrote in their product brochure: "The [XYZ] Switch is one of the most reliable digital switches available for wireless systems today. According to the FCC's ARMIS report, the [XYZ] switch has the least down-time of any switch used in U.S. networks, exceeding Bellcore's reliability standards by 200%. With an installed base of more than 2,300 switches, the [XYZ] switch currently serves over 72 million lines in 49 countries."

7—Demonstration. We know from all those direct response TV advertisers for cleaning products that demonstrations work. And they work in B2B, too.

My favorite ad of all time was from a company manufacturing a fireproofing compound. The ad was printed on paper treated with the compound, bound into the magazine, and had a coupon for requesting a brochure. The headline of the ad was "Try Burning This Coupon!" The cop told the reader to remove the ad from the magazine and to hold a lighted match to it. The paper burned as long as the match was there. But when the match was removed, the flame went out.

The phrases below facilitate those seven approaches:

Battle-tested
Battle-tested bear spray keeps you safe when hiking—not one of our hundreds of customers has ever been injured by a bear in the woods.

Can you pass?
Can your deodorant pass the "sniff test"?

Demonstrated to
Hartz Flea and Tick Collars have repeatedly demonstrated their ability to keep your dog's fur and skin insect-free.

Depend
Millions of drivers depend on AAA for fast, reliable roadside assistance.

Field-proven
Avblend® lubricant has been field-proven for over 1,000 hours of flight without a single camshaft failure.

Laboratory tested, laboratory testing, laboratory tests
Laboratory tests prove that our piping can withstand harsh chemicals and corrosive acids.

Not what you think

Do you know the heaviest object our tailgate truck lift can raise? Hint: It's not what you think.

Proven

Proven to keep a fire going in your fireplace for up to 4 hours.

Put ____ to the test

Put Stanley Steamer carpet cleaning to the test.

Quality control

All optical components are subject to the most rigorous quality control and inspection procedures.

Rely on, count on

Thousands of homeowners rely on our carbon monoxide detectors to work 24/7 and save lives.

Sample, samples

Taste free samples of our new merlots and chardonnay at our winery all month long.

Shock

You'll be shocked at how warm and lightweight this new winter coat feels, even in freezing weather with brisk winds and no sun.

Shown to

Crest is shown to reduce cavities by up to 90 percent.

Side by side

Mop up spills with Brawny and then your regular paper towel side by side and see for yourself how much more absorbent Brawny is.

Standards

Electrical wiring in every Hovnanian home meets all standards of the National Electric Code.

Take the _____ challenge.

Take the Pestcon termite detection challenge.

Test it, try it, take this simple test

But don't take our word for it. Try it yourself at no cost or commitment of any kind.

The test of time

Glidden paints have withstood the test of time.

Track record

Warren Buffett has a long-term portfolio performance track record that few can match.

Without, without a _____

Solar panel installation that goes off without a hitch.

Convince Others to Accept Claims

It is not enough to say your product is the best. You have to prove its effectiveness, because skeptical readers do not take your word for it. They don't take what you say at face value; you have to convince them to accept your arguments as the truth.

Copy is one tool to get people to believe your claim, especially testimonials, case studies, endorsements, awards, certifications, and test results. Other proof tools include charts, tables, graphs, exploded-view diagrams, photos, online video demonstrations, and performance data.

As crazy as that seems.

This tiny stock could go from $1 to $50 a share within 12 months—as crazy as that seems.

NB. This phrase helps defuse skepticism by acknowledging that the claim seems incredible, but saying that nonetheless it is in fact true.

As seen on TV

The George Foreman Grill—as seen on TV!

Battle-tested

The Jeep Grand Cherokee has been battle-tested on the roughest road conditions.

But wait. There's more.

The free CD gives you five powerful software utilities. But wait. There's more.

NB. "But wait. There's more" is used as a transition between sales points. The idea is to get the reader excited about the next benefit to be discussed.

Choose

Choose a few newcomers for your garden or patio.

Doctors, doctor-recommended

The Doctors' Book of Natural Healing Remedies.

Extensively tested

Extensively tested during network interruptions.

For over _____ years

The world's most popular lager for over 90 years.

Government-approved

A government-approved plan that may shield your portfolio against whipsaw volatility.

NB. Any legal activity or product may be said to be "government-approved," which makes it sounds like an endorsement from Uncle Sam. Of course, to be sure, check with your attorney first!

Harvard doctors, Mayo Clinic doctors

Harvard doctors warn about new skin cancer risk.

Here's the proof

Nothing in its price class beats the Corvette for speed and power—and here's the proof.

Look

Look at what Ford's done for you lately.

Make the difference

7 new features that make all the difference.

Next generation

The next generation of lightweight laptops.

Once difficult—now easy

Managing UNIX data centers—once difficult, now easy.

Patented, patent-pending

The Intech cam follower has a patented design.

Proven performance

The ES-2000 wireless hub has proven its performance in over 5,000 installations worldwide.

Tested

Tested for a continuous 8 hours of operation.

Verified

Each vehicle verified by extensive on-road testing.

You'll believe it when you see it

Roach Motel kills cockroaches so your house can quickly be pest-free. You'll believe it when you look into the trap and see for yourself—roaches check in, but they don't check out.

Organizational Approval

"Organizational approval" means that the product is endorsed or recommended by a large and reputable entity, such as a national brand with a stellar reputation, a respected nonprofit, or a professional association.

Approved

Approved for home use by Public Service and Gas.

Certified, certification

Certified by the American Chiropractic Association.

Endorsed

Endorsed by the American Society for Mechanical Engineering.

Official

The Official Boy Scout Guide to the Outdoors.

Recommended

Recommended by the American Dental Association.

Seal of approval

All appliances come with the Underwriters Lab seal of approval.

See how far we've come

Cutco's Saturday Special: See how far we've come in 70 years.

Certifications

Consumers prefer to deal with vendors that are accredited, licensed, insured, approved, or otherwise certified to do the work for which you hire them. Invoking the certifying body adds another level of endorsement to your product.

Accredited

DEAD accredited school.

Approved

FDA-cleared.

As seen on

As seen on Fox News, CNN, CBS.

FDA

This new antidepressant just got FDA approval.

Good Manufacturing Practice (GMP)

Manufacture of our products takes place in our GMP facility.

ISO 20071

Our plant is ISO 20071-certified.

It seems incredible

It seems incredible that you can offer these signed original etchings—for only $5 each!

Underwriters Laboratories, [UL]

All components in our system are UL-approved.

Measure vs. Previous Iterations

A caveat to my advice on creating comparisons: comparative advertising can be problematic, because competitors can take legal action when you state your product is better or theirs has a certain problem. And generally, it's not a question of who's right; the company that wins is usually the one with the deepest pockets for attorney fees. Also, don't make claims of superiority over another specific product or brand without documentation to back it up.

Much easier is to make a favorable comparison between your current model and design vs. *your own* earlier products, technology, or models. Oddly, consumers find this nearly as convincing as competitive analysis, especially when you use numbers to make the comparison.

Double

Our new Osteon 400 juices at twice the speed of our previous model, the Osteon 350.

Faster, _____ as fast

Our new Osteon 400 juicer is twice as fast as our previous model, the Osteon 350.

Just different enough

The design is just different enough to reduce wind drag by 20% for faster speeds and greater fuel.

More

More stable in wind than our Model 100 Drone.

Outpaces, outperforms

Outperforms last year's model hands down!

Price

We've cut the price of a teeth cleaning by 20%.

Reliable

The most reliable home alarm system we've ever offered.

This time we've really outdone ourselves

We just release version 4.0, and this time we've really outdone ourselves!

Twice

Twice the speed of your current Arris modem.

Disarm Skepticism

In the digital age, prospects are more skeptical than ever. Why? Before the web, skepticism about advertising was fairly common. But at the same time, consumers knew that what marketers said in newspaper and magazines ads, and on TV and radio commercials, was highly regulated and therefore could be trusted more.

But the digital age is the Wild West of copy and content. The best thing about the Internet is that you can post just about anything on your website; the worst thing about the Internet is that you can post just about anything on their websites. So for years, consumers have been especially skeptical about advertising claims made on the Internet.

From long habit, this skepticism still exists. Though in actuality, many email service providers, ad networks, and social media networks have cracked down on advertising. For instance, Facebook currently does not allow claims of making money or losing weight in ads and boosted posts. The negative is that advertisers of certain offers are sharply limited in what they can say online. The benefit is that these limitations force marketers to run ads with less outrageous, and therefore more credible, claims.

Luckily, you have this language to preempt and disarm customers' skepticism:

A great value

Restoring your hardwood floors is a great value, especially when it's time to sell your house.

A memo recently crossed my desk

A memo recently crossed my desk that said I would have to raise my prices. But I said "NO! Not yet."

A real crowd-pleaser

Lady Gaga is a real crowd-pleaser.

A summertime favorite

Rita's Italian Ices are a cool treat and a summertime favorite.

Affordable luxury

A bespoke suit is now an affordable luxury.

Best-seller

A New York Times best-seller.

Certificate of authenticity

Genuine Indian arrowheads come with a Certificate of Authenticity from the American Historical Society.

Certified

Toyota certified preowned vehicle advantage.

Could this be?

Could this be the most potent testosterone pill ever formulated?

Demonstrate

Demonstrate how to shape, shadow, and line your eyes with one do-it-all pencil.

Don't pay one penny

Don't pay one penny till this course turns your mind into a mental magnet.

Don't worry

Don't worry. We won't ask you to buy anything.

Easy, easy to use, easier, the easy way

The Jitterbug Smart voice-activated control is designed to be easy to use from the moment you turn it on.

Experts

Leave your oil change to the experts.

Fits your budget, for any budget

We have a wide selection of new and preowned Toyotas that will fit your budget, especially with low monthly lease options.

For the _____ lover

For the World War II history lover.

Frank

A frank discussion of a subject too often avoided.

Genuine

Genuine Permutit water softeners.

Guaranteed, guarantee

Speak Spanish like a diplomat in thirty days guaranteed or your money back.

If money were no object

If money were no object, would you acquire a vacation home on a peaceful lake?

If you're not satisfied

If you're not satisfied, simply return the product to us, tear up your invoice, and you won't owe us a cent.

Incredible deals

Come to our President's Day sale for incredible deals.

Join millions of satisfied users, users rave about it, listen to what our customers are saying about it, our customers rave about it.

Our customers rave about the Dollar Shave Club.

Laugh, laughed

They laughed when I sat down at the piano—but when I started to play!

Legal, legally, 100% legal

The only investment legally obligated to pay you 18 percent gains by June 15.

Made in America, made in the U.S.A.

Made right here in America for quality and reliability.

Mistake

A Little Mistake That Cost a Farmer $3,000 a Year.

Much sought-after

This limited edition signed lithograph is much sought-after by art lovers everywhere.

Never underestimate

Never underestimate the selling power of a woman.

No

No artificial ingredients and no fillers.

No more

No more bad hair says!

Nothing else to buy
Our "Make Money in Real Estate" course gives you everything you need to succeed in this business. It covers the waterfront—there's nothing else to buy.

Only
Link 8 PCs to your mainframe—only $2,395.

Or your money back
Look lovelier in 10 days . . . or your money back!

Own
Own your perfect escape.

Perhaps you should not
Why should you select Frederick Landscaping? Perhaps you should not.

Raise an eyebrow
Little-known loophole in the IRS can save homeowners up to $3,750. And it won't raise an eyebrow at the IRS.

Sound too good to be true?
Does having a tech job like this, starting at $80,000 a year right out of school, sounds too good to be true?

Track record
The system has a track record of 98.8 percent uptime.

Warranty
Covered for one year under manufacturer's warranty.

Warts and all
We tell our customers everything about the used car they are buying—warts and all.

NB. Revealing one or two minor negatives increases credibility, but it's important to say how the minor problem either doesn't affect performance or that you intend to fix it before the sale.

We believe

We believe there are at least 2 million men in New York who love their wives . . . and want to give them spectacular roses for Easter.

Without

Get instant energy in the morning, without the coffee jitters.

Works perfectly, works beautifully.

Works perfectly, exactly as advertised.

Years of experience

Bornstein Heating has 30 years servicing residential and commercial heating systems for thirty years in Morris County.

NB. Prospects are more confident in companies that have been in business for a decade or more. They reason that if the company has been in business that long, they must be satisfying their customers. If you have been in business for seven years, say "nearly a decade." Five years? Write "half a decade." Twenty-three years? "Nearly a quarter of a century." You get the idea: using the biggest unit of measurement (century vs. years; days vs. hours) makes the time period sound longer, which is what you want when convincing consumers of your long experience.

YOU:

YOU: a best-selling children's book author.

You can't fool

You can't fool drivers about all-weather tires.

You can't lose.

With our 100% money-back guarantee of satisfaction, you can't lose.

Talking Frankly

There is a copywriting technique, popularized by Paul Hollingshead at the American Writers and Artists Inc., called "the barstool technique." Paul explains, "This approach is writing copy that is conversational and frank, like two people sitting at a bar shooting the breeze. One of them has just found out about something great he wants to share with the guy on the other barstool, because he's so excited and enthusiastic about what he has learned—and he wants other people to know about and benefit from it just like he has."

You can disarm skepticism by talking frankly—by talking like you're next to your customer at the bar.

Dirty little secret

I'm writing today to share a dirty little secret with you about your phone bill.

Here's the lowdown

Here's the lowdown on the $100 seminar you can take at home—for ten bucks!

Let's talk

Let's talk about life insurance and your family.

May we be frank?

May we be frank about our concern for your home security?

Sick and tired

I'm sick and tired of being ripped off by the high cost of health care—and I want to tell you how I cut my drug and doctor bills in half.

Straight talk

Some straight talk about high-speed Internet connectivity.

What_____ won't tell you, what _____ don't tell you

What your doctor won't tell you about taking statin drugs.

Why haven't more _____ been told these facts?

Why haven't more Mercedes owners been told these facts?

Monetary Guarantee

There are many types of guarantees, including:

- Performance guarantees.
- Service guarantees.
- Satisfaction guarantees.
- Repair guarantees.
- Maintenance guarantees.
- Product delivered is as promised in the ad.
- Delivery guarantees.
- Monetary guarantees.

But among the most effective on converting views to sales is the "monetary guarantee," a guarantee that allows the consumer to return the product for a refund. And there are numerous variations of monetary guarantees:

- Full refund of every penny paid in exchange for return of merchandise to seller.
- Full refund and consumer keeps the product.
- Full refund of every penny paid when customer returns merchandise, *plus* merchant pays for return shipping or picks up the product to be returned from your home or office for free.

- "Product refund"—refund of the product purchase price but no refund of shipping and handling costs.
- Unconditional refund—you get your money back regardless of condition in which the product is returned.
- Conditional refund—given only when product is returned undamaged.
- Proof of fair use—the customer must provide some sort of proof that she gave the product a fair try (e.g., for a home correspondence course, she must show that she completed the assignments).
- Performance refund—money back when the customer is dissatisfied with how well the product works.
- Keeper premiums—you return the product, get a refund, but keep any bonus gifts, premiums, or incentives received free.
- Prorated—For a membership, subscription, or installment payments, you return the product or cancel the service, and as soon as you do, you may stop making monthly payments without penalty of any kind.
- Time-limited refund—guarantee specifies the amount of time within which the customer must return the product to get a refund; typical terms are 30 days, 60 days, and 90 days.
- Lifetime guarantee—product is guaranteed to last for life, and if it falls apart from wear and age, a replacement is sent, either with no charge or for just the shipping fee.

Signal that you're offering one with this language:

For any reason, no reason
If you are unhappy for any reason, or for no reason at all, you may return the item for refund.

Guarantee
All Cutco products are backed by the Forever Guarantee.

Money back, or your money back

Satisfaction guaranteed or your money back.

No questions asked

We'll issue a prompt refund—no questions asked.

Or you pay nothing

You must be 100% satisfied or you pay us nothing.

Question or quibble

We'll issue a full refund, without question or quibble.

Satisfaction guaranteed

Satisfaction guaranteed or your money back. And you can keep the first issue absolutely free—our way of saying "thanks" for giving M *magazine a fair try.*

That way, you risk nothing.

If you are unhappy for any reason, or for no reason at all, you may return the item for refund. That way, you risk nothing.

Thrilled and delighted

You must be thrilled and delighted with your Brookstone vibrating massage chair. If not, just give us a call. We will come pick it up and take it away— and refund all your money.

You can't lose!

If you are unhappy for any reason, or for no reason at all, you may return the item for refund. You can't lose!

You may cancel

You may cancel at any time and receive a refund on the unused portion of your subscription.

Testimonials

Using testimonials—quotations from satisfied customers and clients—is one of the simplest and most effective ways of adding punch and power to brochure, ad, and direct mail copy.

There are no standard words or phrases for testimonials, but instead, here are some helpful guidelines for their use in your copy:

1. Always use real testimonials instead of made-up ones. Even the most skilled copywriter can rarely make up a testimonial that can match the sincerity and credibility of genuine words of praise from a real customer or client. If you ask a customer to give you a testimonial, and he or she says, "Sure, just write something and I'll sign it," politely reply: "Gee, I appreciate that, but would you mind just giving me your opinions of our product—in your own words?" Fabricated or self-authored testimonials (those written by the advertiser or their copywriter) usually sound phony; genuine testimonials invariably have the ring of truth.

2. Prefer long testimonials to short ones. Many advertisers are hooked on using very short testimonials. For instance:

"*. . . fabulous! . . .*"

"*truly funny . . . thought-provoking . . .*"

"*. . . excellent . . . wonderful . . .*"

I believe that when people see these ultrashort testimonials, they suspect that a skillful editing job has masked a comment that was not as favorable as the writer makes it appear. In my opinion, longer testimonials—say, two or three sentences versus a single word or phrase—come across as more believable. For example:

"*Frankly, I was nervous about using an outside consultant. But your excellent service has made me a believer! You can be sure that we'll be calling on your firm to organize all our major sales conferences and other meetings for us. Thanks for a job well done!*"

Sure, it's longer, but it somehow seems more sincere than a one-word superlative. Which brings us to . . . .

3. *Prefer specific, detailed testimonials to general or superlative ones.* Upon receiving a letter of praise from a customer, our initial reaction is to read the letter and find the single sentence that directly praises our company or our product. With a blue pencil, we extract the words we think are kindest about us, producing a bland bit of puffery such as *"We are very pleased with your product."*

Actually, most testimonials would be stronger if we included more of the specific, detailed comments our client has made about how our product or service helped him. After all, the prospects we are trying to sell to may have problems similar to the one our current customer solved using our product. If we let Mr. Customer tell Mr. Prospect how our company came to his rescue, he'll be helping us make the sale. For instance:

"We have installed your new ChemiCoat system in each of our bottling lines and have already experienced a 25 percent savings in energy and material costs. Thanks to your system, we have now added a fourth production line with no increase in energy costs. This has increased profits 15 percent and already paid back the investment in your product. We are very pleased with your product."

Again, don't try to polish the customer's words so it sounds like professional ad copy. Testimonials are usually much more convincing when they are not edited for style.

4. *Use full attribution.* We've all opened direct mail packages that contained testimonials from "J.B. in Arizona" or "Jim S., Self-Made Millionaire." I suspect that many people laugh at such testimonials and think they are phony.

To increase the believability for your testimonials, attribute each quotation. Include the person's name, city and state, and (if a business customer) their job title and company (e.g., "Jim K. Redding, vice president of manufacturing, Divmet Corporation, Fairfield, NJ"). People are more likely to believe this sort of full disclosure than testimonials that seem to conceal the identity of the speaker.

5. *Group your testimonials.* There are two basic ways to present testimonials: you can group them together in one area of your brochure or ad, or you can scatter them throughout the copy. (A third alternative is to combine the two techniques, having many testimonials in a sidebar or separate page, along with a smattering of other testimonials throughout the rest of your copy.)

I've seen both approaches work well, and the success of the presentation depends, in part, on the skill of the writer and the specific nature of the piece. But, all else being equal, I prefer the first approach: to group all your testimonials and present them as a single block of copy. This can be done in a box, on a separate page, or on a separate sheet. My feeling is that when the prospect reads a half dozen or so testimonials, one right after another, they have more impact and power than when the testimonials are separated and scattered throughout the piece.

6. *Get permission.* Make sure you get permission from your customer to reprint his words before including his testimonial in your copy.

I suggest that you send a letter quoting the lines you want to reprint and ask permission to include them in ads, direct mail, brochures, and other materials used to promote your firm. Notice I'm asking for a general release that gives me permission to use the customer's quotation in all current and future promotions, not just a specific ad or letter. This lets me get more mileage out of his favorable comment and eliminates the need to ask permission every time I want to use the quote in a new ad or letter.

7. *Go for quality AND quantity.* While the above guidelines help define what makes a testimonial most effective, the number of testimonials you include is also important. As a rule, have more rather than fewer. Especially on your website, add all new testimonials to your testimonials page.

You may object that no one will read all those testimonials. And you know what? That's okay! When the testimonials go on and on, page after page, with endless scrolling, website visitors are positively influenced by the sheer number of testimonials. They think: if so many people praise this product, it's got to be good!

That being said, I do recommend putting your strongest testimonials at the top of the testimonials page on your site, so visitors at least always read those in full.

Keywords to Engage Customer Trust

According to an article in Target Marketing,[5] "If there is one thing that drives purchases and loyalty, it is *brand trust*. To address the growing trust deficit, companies must learn to be authentic." Authenticity is achieved when you clearly say what you do, do what you said you would do, and then prove that in fact you have done it. The article concludes, "Authenticity only comes together when the organization rallies around the value propositions made to its customers."

Commitment
We have an unshakeable commitment to providing five-star customer service.

Dedicated
Thomson Software is dedicated to making your IT systems meet your CPA's needs.

Excellence, excellent
Old-world craftsmanship ensures excellence in every print job we do for you.

Experts
Our experts have an unmatched reputation for solving boiler problems.

---

5   Shiv Gupta, "Brand Trust in US May Hit Rock Bottom," Target Marketing, 3/19/19.

For over _____

Hold Brothers have been creating tools for profitable option trading for over two decades.

Good hands

You're in good hands with First Mutual.

It's our job

Your total satisfaction is our only job.

Meet your needs, meet your every need

Thomson Software is dedicated to making your IT systems meet your users' needs.

Our customers say

Our customers say the taste of our hand-crafted chocolates is beyond compare.

Over _____ customers

Over 2 million customers buy their tools on Handyman.com.

Over _____ users

Engineered Software has over 15,000 satisfied users.

Promises, promise

We promise to deliver as we have for a quarter of a century.

Repeat business

80% of our orders come from repeat customers.

Since _____

Since 1900, Hershey's has been America's favorite milk chocolate bar.

Trust

7 reasons to trust Unilux to provide superior strobe lighting for your videos and TV commercials.

Unmatched, unduplicated, unparalleled

Our 99.7% customer service rating is unparalleled in the industry.

Uphold

Our dealership upholds the highest stands of delivering service and value.

We do what we say

We do what we say we are going to do—when we say we will do it.

We know

We know a thing or two because we've seen a thing or two.

You can be sure

You can be sure if it's Westinghouse.

Negate Objections

One of the key tasks of both salespeople and copywriters is to negate objections, both those that are voiced by the buyers and those you have reason to suspect they have but are not telling you. Common objections include considerations of:

- Price.
- Terms.
- Warranties.
- Speed of delivery.
- Time required to complete the work.
- Quality.
- Company reputation.

- Compatibility (e.g., does your house have enough electricity to run a large central AC unit?).
- Size (e.g., can the product fit the space available?).
- Service contracts.
- Competitive products.
- Need for the product (e.g., is it a must-have item or a nice-to-have item?).
- No consensus among multiple buyers (e.g., spouses, buying committee).
- Lack of chemistry between buyer and salesperson.
- Brand awareness or reputation.
- Safety.
- Noise.
- Cost of operation.
- Environmentally friendly.

You can preempt those objections with phrases such as:

A great value

Restoring your hardwood floors is a great value, especially when it's time to sell your house.

A memo recently crossed my desk

A memo recently crossed my desk that said I would have to raise my prices. But I said, "NO! Not yet."

Affordable luxury.

A bespoke suit is now an affordable luxury.

Demonstrate

Demonstrate how to shape, shadow, and line your eyes with one do-it-all pencil.

Don't worry

Don't worry. We won't ask you to buy anything. At least not yet.

Easy, easy to use, easier, the easy way

The Jitterbug Smart is designed to be easy to use from the moment you turn it on.

Fit your budget, for any budget

We have a wide selection of new and preowned Toyotas that will fit your budget, especially with low monthly lease options.

Genuine

Genuine Permutit water softeners.

If money were no object

If money were no object, would you acquire a vacation home on a peaceful lake?

If you're not satisfied

If you're not satisfied, simply return the product to us, tear up your invoice, and you won't owe us a cent.

Incredible deals

Come to our President's Day sale for incredible deals.

Legal, legally, 100% legal

The only investment legally obligated to pay you 181% gains by June 15.

Made in America, made in the U.S.A.

Made right here in America for quality and reliability.

No

No artificial ingredients.

No more

No more bad hair days!

Nothing else to buy

Our "Make Money in Real Estate" course gives you everything you need to succeed in this business. It covers the waterfront—there's nothing else to buy.

Or your money back

Look lovelier in ten days . . . or your money back!

Own

Own your perfect winter escape.

> **NB.** *Buy* is a negative word because it means spending money; *own* is a positive alternative, because it means having something you want.

Perhaps you should not

Why should you select Frederick Landscaping? Perhaps you should not.

Raise an eyebrow

Little-known loophole in the IRS can save homeowners up to $3,750. And it won't raise an eyebrow at the IRS.

Sounds too good to be true

A 7-day cruise at this price sounds too good to be true—but it can be yours this summer if you act quickly.

Track record

The system has a track record of 98.8% uptime.

Without

Get instant energy in the morning, without the coffee jitters.

Works perfectly, works beautifully

Works perfectly, exactly as advertised.

You can't lose.

With our 100% money-back guarantee of satisfaction, you can't lose.

Years of experience

Bornstein Heating has 30 years servicing residential and commercial heating systems for thirty years in Morris County.

Educate the Consumer

Give the reader useful information. Years ago, Duncan Hines ran an ad in women's magazines about its chocolate cake mix. The headline was "The secret to moister, richer chocolate cake." Why was that headline so effective? Because it implied you would learn something useful just by reading the ad, regardless of whether or not you bought the product.

Generic advice won't cut it in content marketing today. The prospect does not want to read the same old information he's seen a dozen times before repeated in your next white paper.

Chances are, you possess proprietary knowledge about your product and its applications. Share some of this knowledge in your white papers. Give your reader specific advice and ideas that everyone else isn't already telling him.

Don't be afraid that by telling too much, you'll eliminate the prospect's need for your product or service. Quite the opposite: when they learn the effort that solving their problem entails, and see that you clearly have the needed expertise, they will turn to you for help. In his book *Simple Truths* (MJF Books), Kent Nerburn writes, "The true measure of your education is not what you know, but how you share what you know with others."

Deliver genuine value. When you can, include some highly practical, actionable tips the prospect can implement immediately. The more valuable your content is to prospects, the more readily your content marketing program will achieve its stated objective. It's like fast food stands giving away food samples at the mall: the better the free food tastes, the more likely the consumer is to purchase a snack or meal.

Outline the characteristics, features, and specifications the prospect should look for when shopping for products in your category. If you do this credibly, the prospect will turn your white paper into a shopping list. And of course, the requirements you outline fit your product to a tee. For example, if your white paper title is "Ten things to look for when buying a static mixer," your mixer naturally will have all ten characteristics, while the competition won't.

The goal of education is to generate action or change belief. Content marketing is successful when it gets prospects to take action or changes their opinion, attitude, or beliefs about you and your product as it relates to their needs. Keywords like these will help:

A short course

A short course in railroading.

Advice

Advice to wives whose husbands don't save money—by a wife.

Alert

Driver's alert: Driving can expose you to more dangerous glare than any sunny day at the beach can.

Answer, answers

7 questions to ask before you buy a new table saw—and one good answer to each.

Art, art and science

The Art of Selling Merchandise on Amazon.

Awful

The awful truth about your digestive system and kale.

Boost, boosted

How Howard Thomas Corporation licked the problem of operator inexperience and boosted production 77%.

Choice, choose

How to choose the ideal material for your deck: cedar or pine?

Discover

Discover stories of intrigue.

Do you know?

Do you know the hidden dangers of locating your propane gas tanks too close to your house?

Everything you need to know, you need

Everything you need to know about the Jersey shore.

Forget about

Forget about marriage . . . why not just get engaged?

Here's what

Here's what you may not know about inspecting your tires for wear . . .

Here's why

Here's why seals and bearings of TFE-fluorocarbon resins may be your solution.

How

How fortunes are really built in today's market.

How to

How to solve all your money problems forever!

It's like getting an MBA in only _____ months

Taking our training is like getting an MBA is only 3 months!

> **NB.** The above is an example of a persuasion technique called "transubstantiation." Transubstantiation entails making it sound as if what you are selling is practically equivalent to something better. This is a concept from Christianity, where wine becomes the blood of Christ and a wafer his body. In transubstantiation for persuasive writing, you use words to make something seem more than it is. A classic example was the old comic book ad selling "sea monkeys" as "instant pets." What you got was in fact not monkeys or pets, but rather, a vial of dried brine shrimp eggs, along with instructions for hatching them.

Know

What everybody ought to know about this stock-and-bond business.

Learn

Learn at home in your spare time.

Lessons

Become a master angler in 3 easy lessons.

Little-known

Why haven't more drivers been told these little-known facts about making their brake drums last longer?

Make it pay, make it pay for you

Almost everyone has a $100,000 idea. Here's how to make it pay.

Myths

The 3 big replacement window myths.

One simple thing

Do this one simple thing and make knee pain disappear.

Promotes

Promotes hair growth from within.

Quick tips for_____

Quick tips for housebreaking your new puppy.

Right and wrong

Right and wrong ways of betting the horses.

Secrets of, the secret of, secret

The secret to getting all the credit you ever wanted—even if you've been bankrupt.

The amazing secret

The Amazing Diet Secret of a Desperate Shipping Clerk from Ohio.

The _____ biggest mistakes

The 5 biggest mistakes when investing in gold and how to avoid each.

The Case

The case of the crumpled letter.

The complete guide to _____

The complete guide to flipping houses for fun and profit.

The good, the bad, and the ugly

Variable annuities: the good, the bad, and the ugly.

The quick and easy way to _____

The quick and easy way to write and sell ebooks for fun and profit.

Things to look for
Things to look for in judging people.

Three easy steps (or any other number)
Three easy steps to fine wood finishing.

Tips
Winter Driving Safety Tips.

Warning
Warning: avoid this dubious investment advice at all cost.

Ways, new ways
8 ways to give back without giving money.

What everybody ought to know
What everybody ought to know about this stock-and-bond business.

Why
Why men need to get a prostate exam annually.

Why don't
Why don't more casino gamblers know these tricks for beating the house?

You
YOU: a successful house flipper.

You can do
You can do much more than you think.

You know
You know you want a subzero fridge.

You may think

You may think all pain relievers are the same. Your doctor doesn't.

> **NB.** If you are correct and the prospect is in fact thinking what you have guessed he is thinking, you almost surely have him hooked, because here you are entering into the conversation he is having in his mind about his experience with pain relievers that don't work.

Convey New Information

Educating consumers by providing new and useful information is a marketing tactics that has been around for decades. Today, it has been given its own name: "Content marketing." And its use has increased geometrically in recent years.

Content marketing—giving away free information to build your brand, increase response to marketing campaigns, convert more online traffic, and educate the prospect on your technology, methodology, products, services, and applications—is one of the hot trends in marketing today.

The term "content marketing" may have been coined in 1996, at a roundtable for journalists held at the American Society of Newspaper Editors, by John F. Oppendahl, making the terminology over two decades old. But in fact, content marketing has been used for far longer than that. It's only the name that is of recent vintage, not the method. I personally have been doing content marketing for four decades, and some marketers have been at it even longer.

Today, more attention is being focused on content as a marketing tool than ever. For instance, in August 2017, Apple announced the company was making a $1 billion investment in original content.[6] Forrester forecasts that by 2023, annual digital marketing spend will reach $146 billion.[7] More than nine out of ten business-to-business

---

6   Content Marketing Institute, 8/26/17.
7   https://www.marketingdive.com/news/forrester-digital-marketing-spend-to-reach
    -146b-by-2023-but-search-lands/549285/

companies use content marketing.[8] They utilize phrases like these to educate consumers:

A _____'s Guide
An engineer's guide to measuring large loads.

Analysis, analyze
Monthly stock market analysis with updated model portfolio in every issue.

Authoritative
The authoritative source on insurance underwriting.

Be aware of _____
Be aware of the pending change in Medicare that could affect your coverage.

Educate, educational
Get an education in annuities at our next retirement workshop.

Eye-popping, eye-opening
Eye-opening news about commercial space travel.

Habits
5 habits of winning traders.

Have you heard?
Have you heard the good news about pancreatic cancer treatment?

Idea, Ideas
A new idea for homeowners who want to cut their electric bills without installing ugly solar panels on the roof.

---

8   AWAI, The Writer's Life, 2/27/19.

Information
A wealth of information on trading awaits—yours for the asking.

Inside, insider
Get the facts on this huge stock buyback from company insiders—100% legal.

Insight
New insights into electroplating.

Instructions, instruction, instructive
Practical instruction on the art of negotiation.

Keep up, keep in touch
Keep up with the latest developments in aerospace technology.

Lesson
An important lesson for seniors: how to avoid slips and falls.

Let you in
I want to let you in on a little secret about microwave radiation and airport radar.

Mystery, unlock the mystery, take the mystery out of _____
Take the mystery out of how to win at the stock market.

New FREE Report
New FREE Report shows how to keep your money in your IRA . . . and out of Uncle Sam's hands.

Perspective
A fresh perspective on keeping wild animals as pets.

Questions

Questions to ask when your doctor prescribes a new medication.

Shocking

The shocking truth about getting into a hot tub with strangers.

Stay abreast of, stay in the know

Stay abreast of new developments in the American electrical grid.

Straight talk

Some straight talk about getting the best modems and router for your home network.

Strategies, strategy

Winning option selling strategies from a master trader!

Surprise

What's the one vegetable you should never eat? The answer may surprise you.

Thought-provoking

Thought-provoking advice on parenting your ADHD, OCD, or autistic child.

Tips

21 tips to help you lose weight.

Trick, tricks

Learn Jill's simple trick that helped her lose 17 pounds in 8 weeks.

Ways

10 Ways YouTube Can Save You Money on Do-It-Yourself Projects.

What every _____ should/ought to know about _____

What every investment advisor should know about universal life insurance.

What NOT to do

What not to do when your car hydroplanes . . .

What they won't tell you, what they don't teach you, what you won't learn

What you won't learn about entrepreneurship and small business at Harvard Business School.

Why you should not

Why, when a small animal runs into the road in front of your car, you should NOT swerve to avoid hitting it.

Correct Misconceptions

Educating readers by correcting misconceptions is a four-step process. First, use keywords such as the ones below to inform them that what they believe or think is in fact not correct.

Second, tell them specifically what part of their thinking, believe system, or attitude is wrong. No one is wrong about everything. Let them know their misconception is about just one thing.

Third, tell them the correct information. And fourth, offer lots of proof to support your argument to overcome skepticism, disbelief, and resistance to having long held misconceptions challenged.

Absolutely absurd

What most people have been taught about portfolio diversification is absolutely absurd.

Awful truth

The awful truth about men over 50 and testosterone.

Bad idea

Buying options is a bad idea . . . but selling them is a great idea!

B.S.

Has your high-priced dentist been feeding you a load of B.S. about dental implants?

Bunk!

Siding salesmen tell you a lot of bunk—here's what can really protect the exterior of your home while looking good doing it!

Common questions, frequently asked questions

6 common questions about long-term care—and one good answer to each.

Contrary to popular belief

Contrary to popular belief, strawberries are not a fruit!

Despite what you've heard

Despite what you've heard, fracking is a safe oil recovery technology.

Dos and don'ts

Dos and don'ts of lifting heavy weights on the job or at the gym.

Mysteries

Solve the new tax law mysteries.

Myths

Debunking myths about Irish culture.

What ____ didn't tell you about _____

What your doctor didn't tell you about ingrown toenails.

Why so many

Why so many people lose money trading commodities.

Guides and Reports

Many consumers and business prospects are information seekers. They like to do their own research, and by the time they contact a salesperson, the typical B2B prospects have done 80 percent of his product investigation, mainly online.

Offering guides and reports has several benefits. First, it aids the prospect by helping him with his product research. Second, because you wrote it, the guide or report naturally favors your technology, design, or methodology, even though it does not blatantly sell your specific product in most cases. So it predisposes him to like what you are going to try to sell to him.

Third, prospects appreciate free guides, and providing them to customers creates valuable goodwill that makes them a bit more willing to give your emails and other communications some of their time and attention. Fourth, publishing free useful content helps build your reputation as an expert in your industry. And all else being equal, people gravitate toward doing business with knowledgeable pros instead of those whom they perceive as just salespeople. Present yourself as such.

Ebook
New ebook is the perfect beginner's guide to investing in cryptocurrencies.

Guide
Travel and vacation guide to Italy—yours FREE!

Manual
The World's Most Valuable Money Manual and Course.

New report
New Report Highlights Risk of Using Unknown Mobile Security Apps.

New study
New Study Reveals That Surgery May Not Actually Relieve Knee Pain.

Podcast

Join us Tuesday for our live podcast on retirement living.

The Little Black Book of

The Little Black Book of Momentum-Trading Secrets.

Tip sheet

Tip sheet reveals how to save money on your medications.

Top

Top 10 team-building ideas.

Ultimate

The Ultimate Guide to Windows Server on Azure.

Video, DVD

New video shows how to read price charts with up to 90% accuracy.

Ways

Seven ways employers can support employee caregivers.

Webinar

New free webinar reveals little-known online advertising secrets.

White paper

Free white paper: Managing UNIX Data Centers.

Provide Proof

As I've mentioned, it's not enough to just say something about your product—you have to *prove* it. Beyond the strategies already discussed for presenting approvals, certifications, and other testimonials, here are some more methods for educating the consumer through proof (and the language to do so):

- **Social proof:** many other people are buying it and like it and give you testimonials to that effect.
- **Business proof:** top companies or individuals in the industry like, recommend, or use it.
- **Product proof:** a feature and benefit your product has that others do not.
- **Quantitative proof:** graphs, charts, statistics, test results, field performance, and data that demonstrate superiority.
- **Expert proof:** the person or organization that makes the product or renders the service is a proven expert in the field—or else the product is recommended by experts.
- **Scientific proof:** experimental results published in scientific journals.
- **Clinical proof:** results from clinical trials published in peer-reviewed medical journals.
- **Anecdotal evidence:** things that either happened to you or you heard secondhand.

#1 Seller/selling, best-seller, the largest-selling
America's #1-selling weight loss supplement.

Ancient
Ancient secrets: Diamond Dowsing.

Blocking
The UV-blocking sun shirt with UPF 50+sun protection.

Clinical studies
247 clinical studies agree that lutein helps improve vision.

Details

Details inside!

Each month

Each month, more than 5 million readers pick up the latest issue of our magazine.

Everything

Everything you ever wanted to know about sex but were afraid to ask.

Facts

Why haven't more condo owners been told these important facts?

Good reasons

7 good reasons to use Sensodyne toothpaste.

Here's why

Here's why more PC users choose Norton Antivirus.

Just one more thing

Just one more thing you should know about hydroponic gardening.

Let's take a look

Let's take a look at the reasons why you should not be eating kale . . .

Makes good sense

Switching from oil to gas heat makes good sense.

More reasons why

And there are even more reasons to switch to Verizon Wireless.

No wonder

No wonder mining engineers call Continental Conveyor to handle the biggest loads.

Not one ____ in a _____

Pears so rare that not one person in a thousand has even tasted them!

Outperforms, outclasses, outsells

Outperforms every other model in its class.

Preferred by_____

Preferred by hobbyists nationwide.

Quite a package

Power steering. Rearview camera. Automatic accident avoidance. All in all, quite a package. And it all comes standard!

Raving

Everywhere women are raving about this amazing new shampoo!

Recommended

Dermatologist-recommended for scars and stretch marks.

Seeing is believing

If seeing is believing, take a look at these pictures.

_____ that works

Weight loss that works.

Top

Top dentists brush with Crest.

Unbelievable as it may seem

The new iPhone can be powered up anywhere, anytime without a charger, as unbelievable as it may seem.

Used by

Used by professional land surveyors in 32 countries!

World's best-kept secret
Are these delicious 100% sugar-free cookies the world's best-kept secret for diabetics?

You never saw
You Never Saw Such Letters As Harry and I Got About Our Pears.

You'll be amazed
You'll be amazed at how quick and easy it is to make fresh juice from fruits and vegetables.

Verify Performance

"Performance" refers to how well a product can do the thing it was designed to do. "Verify performance" means offer proof or support for your product performance claims.

Availability
97.5% system availability of 97.5 percent helps you avoid costly downtime.

Completely satisfying
Buying a Hovnanian home is a completely satisfying experience from free initial design consultation to final product.

Critically acclaimed
Critically acclaimed performance.

Difference
There's a big difference in floor absorbents—test it for yourself.

Fast, faster, fastest
Find hard disk files fast!

Find out for yourself

Find out for yourself which antifoaming agent works best.

For over_____

Blue Star has been helping small businesses get the money they need for over three decades.

Gets the job done

Blue Ribbon lawn fertilizer gets the job done.

Half-price

Special half-price get-acquainted offer for a hard-to-believe introductory $32.45.

How, how to

How Hercules helps . . .

How I_____

How I Improved My Memory in One Evening.

Is your product easily damaged?

Are your product shipments easily damaged? Bemis flexible packaging may solve your problem.

ISO-certified

All components are manufactured in our ISO-certified fabrication unit.

Prove, proven

Doctors prove 2 out of 3 women can have more beautiful skin in fourteen days.

Rated, ranked

Rated the #1 hospital in New Jersey.

Retains, retained

Pierced by 301 nails . . . retains full air pressure.

Tested

Thoroughly tested for water resistance.

The official _____ of _____

The official breakfast cereal for U.S. Olympic teams.

The oldest

Brewed since 1929, the oldest beer in the United States.

Vetted

All courses are vetted by top professors in their fields.

Without a single failure

6,000 systems installed in the field without a single failure!

Create Consumer Confidence in Your Company or Brand

In addition to emotions, needs, and wants, the reputation of the seller also influences consumer purchase decisions. For instance, in Information Technology, there was for many years a popular saying among IT professionals: "No IT manager ever got fired for buying an IBM computer that didn't work."

What it means is that IBM's leadership position in the computer industry meant businesses trusted IBM to meet their computing needs efficiently and reliably. So if there was a problem with the hardware, and the CEO complained, the IT manager only had to say, "But it's an IBM," and his job would be safe.

Back in the day, IBM was the leader in mainframe computing. RCA decided to get into the business and take market share away from IBM.

So RCA built a mainframe that many believed offered superior performance to the IBM mainframes at a lower price.

But instead of flying out of the factory, the RCA mainframes sat gathering dust on the loading dock, never sold in any significant volume, and were soon phased out. Why? The answer is simple.

Having a mainframe fail spelled major disaster. But if it was an IBM mainframe, the IT manager was not to blame; he had made the safe and wise choice buying on IBM with its stellar reputation. However, if the mainframe went down and the CEO stormed into the IT manager's office and yelled, "Why the heck did you buy our mainframe from RCA and not IBM?" the IT manager could expect to find himself out on the street.

In a similar way, on Wall Street there is a saying, "No portfolio manager ever got fired for buying a blue chip stock that went down in share price." The reputation of the merchant, manufacturer, or other seller reassures and comforts consumers and, in business marketing, helps protect the buyer's reputation, career, and job security. Some simple language adjustments allow you to do it, too.

Best-known
The best-known shop for muffler and brake repairs.

Class, in its class
The Apple Watch Series 4 is in a class by itself.

Dominant, dominate
Epner Technologies dominated the electroplating industry for high-tech applications and precision machine parts for many years.

For over _____
Wells & Drew has been providing fine engraved letterhead to law firms for over a century.

Great, greatest

Harley-Davidson makes the greatest motorcycles on Earth.

Icon, iconic

Schweppes is an iconic brand in sparkling and tonic waters.

Known for

Known for our quality and attention to detail.

Leading

Amazon is the world's leading e-commerce company.

Legendary

Legendary Mercedes engineering and performance.

Number one

Coke: number one in the global soft drink market.

Preferred by

Mack Trucks are preferred by transportation professionals nationwide.

Regarded, well regarded

My father used to say, "They are well regarded in the advertisements."

Renowned

Ray's is renowned for making the best pizza in the Village!

Respected

The most respected cancer center in the New York metropolitan area: Memorial Sloan Kettering.

Revered

Jack Daniels is revered as a premiere maker of fine whiskey.

Top-rated, top-ranked
Fossler is the top-rated printer of gold and silver seals in the business today.

Who else
Who can protect your computers from hacker attacks better than Norton Antivirus?

World-class
A world-class 5G network for voice, video, and data communication.

CHAPTER 6

Convert Call to Actions into Sales Revenue

Your request for response—whether you are seeking a lead or offering a free download or an opt-in—is known as the Call to Action, or CTA. And the CTA that makes the most money is convincing the prospect to click the Order Now button or call your toll-free number.

The two big failures of most modern advertising, says Sergio Zyman in his book *The End of Marketing As We Know It*, are (a) to forget to give reasons to buy and (b) *to forget to ask for the sale.*

We've all seen the ads that "raise brand awareness" without ever implying that there's something to buy.

Even Coke had them. Depending on how old you are, you might remember. In 1979, Coke ran its famous "Hilltop" campaign. Kids from all over the world gathered to sing, "I'd like to teach the world to sing." The soft drink or what it did for you on a hot day had barely anything—even nothing—to do with the ad.

"I actually loved that film," says Zyman, "It's touching, warm, and a great vehicle to promote unity among the different people of the world. . . . But did that ad sell any more Coke? Nope." In fact, during that period of award-winning, warm and fuzzy advertising, Coca Cola actually *lost* market share.

This general language is proven effective and popular among copywriters and marketers when putting together CTAs. More targeted language for CTA strategies are below:

Application, apply
Simple application.

Ask for _____
Ask for a free DVD on how to overcome your addiction and get clean at the Recovery Center.

Bet
Bet on this metal to rally in the electric vehicle revolution.

Buy, buy direct
Buy $100,000 life insurance you can afford.

Choose
Choose your deal today—good, better, or best!

Claim
Just claim your favorite deal below.

Click, click here, click now
To claim your free bottle of Provarin, click here now.

Experience
Experience Lands' End.

Find
Find a new favorite to love.

Free information

Free information by mail.

Get

Get the Facts—FREE!

Hurry

Hurry while supplies last.

Meet

Meet former TV personality and talk show host from The View *Elisabeth Hasselbeck March 27, 7p.m., at Books & Greetings.*

Order now

To order now, just click the button below.

Reply today

Reply today and get a free sample of our incredible foam mattress.

Scan

Scan this code to buy now.

Take a few seconds, take a few days

Take a few seconds and you may save on taxes.

Train

Train at home.

Try it, try it on

Try it before you buy it.

Treat Yourself

Victoria's Secret: Treat Yourself & Score.

Generate Leads

"Lead generation" is a marketing technique that seeks to generate an inquiry rather than an immediate sale. Lead generation is also known as "two-step" marketing, because there are two steps: (1) generating the lead and (2) converting the lead to a sale. "One-step" marketing by comparison makes the sale directly. Example: direct response TV ads in which you call a toll-free number and order the product directly over the phone.

Just so we are clear, let's define the key terms of lead-generating marketing:

- *Inquiry*—an inquiry is a request for more information about your product or service, without regard to whether the inquirers are legitimate potential buyers or have any real interest in what you sell.
- *Lead, sales lead*—an inquiry from a qualified prospect.
- *Qualified prospect*—a potential customer with the money and authority to buy what you are selling; either a strong desire to own the product, a need the product can fill, or a problem the product or service can solve; and ideally some added degree of urgency to get the need addressed or the problem taken care of.
- *Lead quantity*—the total number of leads generated by a marketing campaign or promotion.
- *Lead quality*—a measure of how good the lead is based on a combination of the prospect's desirability as a potential customer or client combined with how likely they are to become a customer or client of your firm (see the lead ranking section later in this chapter for a more precise discussion of quality).

There are five factors that determine lead quality and separate the qualified prospects from the tire kickers; these are defined by the formula MAD-FU as follow:

- *Money.* They have a large enough budget to afford what you are selling.
- *Authority.* They have the authority to spend that money on your product.
- *Desire.* They very much need or want what you are selling. Either they covet the product or have an essential need or important problem your product can solve.
- *Fit.* There is an excellent fit between what your product does and what the prospect needs it for.
- *Urgency.* They prospect is eager to buy. They want the product soon or even immediately. They need it for a current application, not a future use.

"Hard leads" are prospects who want to talk to a salespeople to get answers to questions, see a product demonstration, or get a proposal or price quotation.

A "soft" lead may be someone requesting free content, a free gift, a free product brochure, or other product information. They may satisfy some of the MAD-FU criteria, but not all.

Soft leads never have urgency. Without urgency, the salesperson's job is much more difficult. With urgency, he is more likely to make the sale.

A prospect without urgency but with a future need is a good lead if they meet two of the other categories out of MAD-F. For instance, if they have the money to purchase and authority to do so, you have a chance of converting them from a prospect to a buyer. If they lack money, authority, and desire, they are a poor lead and unlikely to close.

Usually, we operate between the two extremes and adjust the lead flow and quality to meet immediate needs in the marketplace and to satisfy the concerns of the sales organization.

Exactly what kind of leads are needed will vary at times. Sometimes there will be too many that don't pan out into sales. Other times there won't be enough leads to keep the sales staff busy. Luckily, I've included a few different types of language to employ:

Act now
Act now and get 25% off.

Appointment
Go on our website and view the online calendar to schedule your free appointment with one of our precious metals experts today.

Be one of the first
Be one of the first 100 callers . . .

Brochure
Send for our free 16-page color brochure.

Call, call toll-free
Call the toll-free number now.

Click here now
To download your free manual, just click here now.

Clip
Just clip and complete the coupon and drop it in the mail.

Demo
Take an online demo of our software.

Do this, do it now, do it today, do it right now
Do this, and you'll never overpay for gas again.

Drop, just drop

Just fill out the reply card and drop it in the mail.

Enter

Enter our drawing today.

Estimate

Call today for a free, no-obligation estimate for landscaping your yard.

Everything to gain

Why not request your free kit today? You have everything to gain. And you won't pay us even one thin dime.

Everywhere

You'll find Masonite Pressed Foods everywhere. Go online to find the nearest store.

Explore

Explore Charleston.

Facts

Get the facts—FREE!

Fastest service, for fast service

Want faster service? Call our toll-free number now.

Free

The information is free. And there's no obligation.

Go

Go modular for your next clean air project—send for our catalog today.

Hurry

But you must hurry. We have printed only so many winter insulation guides—no more.

If you will let me

I want to send you some valuable information on starting your own business in your spare time. If you will let me.

Information Kit, _____ Kit

Have an idea for an invention? Call now to get our free Inventor's Kit.

Inquiry, inquiries

Inquire now while plots are still available.

Instantly yours

Click the Next Step button today, and the free ebook is instantly yours.

Invite, invitation

I invite you to call today for a free, no-obligation estimate by phone.

Just one more thing …

There's just one more thing I want to share with you.

Keep this under your hat, keep it under your hat

Keep this free offer under your hat. Do not share it with friends. It is for our preferred customers.

Last chance

Last chance to claim your catalog and $10 savings certificate!

Look forward

We look forward to receiving your reply.

Mail the coupon

Mail the coupon for your free samples.

May we?

May we send you the facts, figures, and statistics to help you make on intelligent buying decision?

Needs assessment

Come in today for a free needs assessment that shows at which age you'll have enough money to retire secure for life.

Nothing to lose, you can't lose

Do go ahead. Make the call. You can't lose!

Quote

Send us your dimensions and other specifications today for a free quote.

Request

Request our new product guide today.

Reserve

Reserve your seats today.

Review

One of our agents will come to your home and review all your current insurance policies and coverage at no cost to you.

Risk-free, no-risk

There's no risk. And no obligation to buy.

Samples

Call for your free samples today. Operators are standing by.

See for yourself

Send for our FREE DVD today—and see how quickly and easily you can have a flat, toned stomach!

See us today

Come right down to the showroom and see us today.

Send, send for

Send for valuable free information on fencing for your yard.

Standing by

Call for your free samples today. Operators are standing by.

Stop

Stop roof leaks with FlexTape—send for a FREE sample roll.

Take a step, take the next step

Take a step in the right direction.

Test

Free eye test chart just like your eye doctor's for at-home vision check.

Urgent, urgently, urge

The Army needs nurses—urgently. Visit your local recruitment center today.

We're waiting, we look forward

We're waiting for your call.

With your approval, with your OK, with your permission

With your permission, I want to send you some free stamps from Latin America for your collection. No cost or obligation, of course.

Without cost

This massive 288-page product guide and data book is yours free, without cost or obligation of any kind.

You can't lose

So click the button below and download your free special investor's report now. You can't lose.

You'll be glad you did!

So click the button below and download your free special investor's report now. You'll be glad you did!

Effective Imperative Keywords

"Imperatives" are commands that tell the reader to take a specific action. And imperatives work in sales copy. For instance, the simple imperative headline "Buy Scott Towels" ran repeatedly in newspapers years ago, and Scott would not have made so many repeat insertions unless the ad was working. Here are some to use:

Accept no _____

Use Firestone Tires. Accept no second-rate brands.

Buy

Buy Scott Towels.

Come, come to

Come to Outback for our new steak and shrimp on the barbie special!

Don't delay

We expect these remainder items to sell out fast. So don't delay. Order now. Once they're gone, it's too late.

Eat

Eat at the Tip-Top Diner tonight!

Join

Join Massage Envy today and get your first massage free!

Listen

Listen to this important news about the latest breakthrough in treating Alzheimer's.

Make

Don't have the time to work out? Then we urge you to make the time. Here's why . . .

Pass this message on

Pass this message on to anyone who's interested in staying ahead of the competition.

Register now, sign up today

Register Now: How to Manage Fake News in the Real World.

Stop

Stop.

Take charge of your life, take charge of your future

Enroll at Apex Tech and take charge of your life, your income, and your future today.

Offering Autonomy to Customer

Do you dislike shopping for a new car because, as soon as you step foot into the dealership, multiple salespeople, all competing with one another for the opportunity to sell a car, descend on you like a kettle of vultures?

While some consumers actively seek help and service from a sales-person, others dislike salespeople and being sold. For these consumers, offering them the autonomy to shop undisturbed and make their own selection can bring them back to your business again and again and make you their preferred vendor.

The iconic example of a business offering consumer autonomy was the Horn & Hardart chain of "Automats." In these self-service restaurants, popular with the New York City lunch crowd in the first half of the 20th century, sandwiches and other meals were displayed in glass-covered compartments. There were no waiters. You self-serviced by browsing through the windows, making your selection, putting the appropriate coinage into a slot, which then unlocked the compartment window, enabling you to remove your food and bring it to one of the self-seating tables.[9]

Today, the increasing number of self-service kiosks, checkout lines, and buffet restaurants attests to the continued popularity of and growing desire for consumer autonomy. Have that autonomy reflected in your copy:

Browse, browse to your heart's desire
Browse our thousands of used books in peace and solitude.

By yourself, all by yourself
Choose the tiles that fit your design by yourself.

Do it
Nike. Just do it.

Don't depend
Don't depend on strangers to take care of faulty wiring. Call Con Edison instead.

---

9   https://www.6sqft.com/horn-and-hardart-automats-redefining-lunchtime-dining
-on-a-dime/

Hassle-free
Hassle-free shopping with no pesky salesperson bothering you.

Make up your own mind
Walk our showroom undisturbed and make up your own mind.

No sales pressure
Pick the kitchen countertop that fits your design and your budget—no sales pressure.

No salesperson will call, no salesperson will visit
Send for our free brochure today. No salesperson will call.

On your own
Make your purchase decision on your own.

Self-service
Pump your own gas at New Jersey's biggest self-service gas station.

Shop
Shop to your heart's content. Look as long as you want.

Undisturbed
Make your selection undisturbed by sales reps unless you ask for their assistance.

You're the boss
When you own a Baskin Robbins franchise, you're the boss!

Get People to Say Yes

Ultimately, the goal of the copywriter is to get people to say yes to the offer, the product, the solution, the idea, the service, or the methodology you propose.

Of course, many prospects will say no. But here's a secret professional salespeople and marketers know that many others don't. In most instances, you only need a small percentage of your prospects, often in the single digits, to say yes—and still have a wildly profitable business. Use these words and phrases to get qualified prospects to say yes, and don't agonize over all the noes you hear to get to those valuable few buyers who say yes:

Exploring

Start exploring. Choose a National Geographic *magazine that is right for you!*

Go ahead

Puddles? Who cares? Go ahead—walk right through them. Waterproof rain boots keep feet dry.

Sweepstakes

You'll be automatically entered into our sweepstakes for a chance to win prizes when you place an order of $25 or more by March 21, 2020.

Talk to us

Need OSHA training? Relax. Talk to us!

Visit

Visit Myrtle Beach—melt the monotony of winter away!

Rhetorical Questions and Statements

A rhetorical question is a question you ask without expecting an answer, usually to make a point. Usually, the answer is glaringly obvious, which helps make your point stand out. It's also a way to get customers to say yes—because it's the only possible response.

"" [quotation marks]

The "totally incorrect" way to make money.

Do you want to have money worries for the rest of your life?

Do you want to have money worries for the rest of your life—or would you prefer lifetime financial security?

How many times?

How many times have you missed out on an idea or opportunity that made others rich?

What else do you need?

What else do you need to make yourself happy?

What's holding you back?

What's holding you back from owning a Mont Blanc fine writing instrument?

Why can't

Why can't a woman be more like a man?

Appeal to Customer Desires

Experienced marketers and salespeople, and even many who are not experienced but know and understand people, either have an instinctive feel for what customers desire—or else can find out by asking them either in person, over the phone, or on a web page that asks qualifying questions.

Some of the more common core desires people have that your products may be able to satisfy, depending on what you are selling, include:

- Love.
- Appreciation.
- Admiration.
- Beauty.
- Creativity.
- Power.
- Respect.
- Being productive.

- Being informed.
- Success.
- Recognition.
- Forgiveness.
- Money.
- Career success.
- Security.
- Leisure time.
- Health.
- Self-esteem.
- Peace of mind.
- Autonomy.
- Pleasure.
- Freedom from pain.
- Prestige.
- Positive self-image.
- Freedom.
- Own their own business.
- Work at home.
- Express their individuality.
- Friendship.
- Companionship.
- Family.
- Be important.
- Travel.
- Fun.
- Do less work.
- Help others.
- Recognition.
- Romance.
- Material possessions.
- Money savings.
- Time.
- Profit.
- Comfort.
- Pleasure.
- Self-improvement.
- A new job.
- Price of ownership.
- Color and style.
- Variety.
- Avoidance of boredom.
- New experiences.
- Getting what they need.
- Getting what they want.
- Luxury.
- Attention.
- Fame.
- Popularity.
- To be influential.

Achieving these goals and fulfilling these desires are among the most powerful and persuasive things you can offer.

Could this be?

Could this be the answer to your prayers?

Desire, desires

Could this fulfill your fondest desires?

Do

Do what you want to do, when you want to do it.

Dreams, dream

Get rich beyond the dreams of avarice.

Friends

How to win friends and influence people.

Get rid of, banish

Get rid of money worries for good.

Get what you want

Get what you want out of life.

Goals

Will this be the year you achieve your most important goals?

Grand Prize, win the grand prize

Grand Prize—a Year of GODIVA.

Happiness

Unlock the secrets to lifetime happiness.

Hope

Now you can do more than just hope for what you want out of life.

Ideal

Could this be the ideal lifestyle for you?

Perfect

The perfect antidote to what ails you.

Settle

Don't settle for second best.

What you are missing, what you have been missing

Visit Ireland and see what you've been missing.

Wishes

Now your wishes can come true!

Worry, worries

Get rid of money worries for good.

Thanking Prospects for Replying or Buying

Finally, when the language in this book has worked—when you acknowledge a request for more information or are sending an order confirmation—thank the prospect for his inquiry or purchase. The reasons to do so in writing are as follows:

- It confirms your receipt of the inquiry or order—which gives the customer reassurance that the request transmitted by him was received by you.
- In the buyer/selling relationship and transaction, the customer believes that in some way he is doing you a favor by patronizing your business. Saying "thank you" acknowledges and confirms the thought already in his mind.
- In an era of haste-based rudeness (e.g., crowded department stores where some sales clerks are rude and offensive, or

in restaurants where your server runs right past your table and pretends not to notice you signaling for service), good manners can go a long way toward building long-term goodwill.

- Older customers especially expect good manners, and all customers appreciate it.
- Thanking the customer in writing is fast, doesn't waste his time, doesn't force him into a conversation he may not want to have, is quick and easy for the merchant, and—if done automatically via email autoresponder—ensures the courtesy of a thank-you is never accidentally omitted or forgotten.
- On the other hand, a handwritten thank-you stands out and feels more personal.
- Also effective in thank-you follow-up is some sort of reinforcement or flattery that they made a good buying decision.
- Too, reinforcing valuable extras in the purchase terms—e.g., in-home technical service, remote monitoring of equipment— shows appreciation while reinforcing the wisdom of the customer's purchase decision and choice of merchant.

Appreciated, much appreciated
Your business is much appreciated.

Congratulations
Congratulations on becoming the owner of a new 2020 Dodge Viper.

Delighted, we're delighted
We're delighted you chose ENT Associates for your health care needs.

Enjoy

Enjoy new vitality and better nutrition by juicing fresh fruits and veggies with your Ostion Juicer.

Here's what's in store, here's what you can expect, here's what's waiting

Here's what's waiting for you as a new AARP member.

I am at, I am here, we are here

We are here to answer your questions and provide all the customer service and support you will ever need.

Member, membership

Club membership has its privileges, which are extended to members only.

Questions?

Questions? Call our customer support team toll-free at 800-XXX-XXXX at any time of the day or night.

Thank you

Thank you for shopping at Bloomingdales.

Thanks _____ and please _____

Thanks for your business and please visit our store again.

We know you have a choice

We know you have a choice of Internet providers; thanks for choosing Optimum.

Welcome

Welcome to Blue Nile as a new customer.

Your business

We thank you for your business.

Your order

Your order has been received and shipped.

You've made a smart choice, you've made a wise choice

You've made a smart choice switching to AT&T as long voice, data, and Internet provider.

Appendix I:
The Discovery Process

The "discovery process" refers to the methods that can help you write great copy for specific products and services.

The many words, phrases, and copy and headline samples in this book may be good models or inspiration or sources of selling ideas.

But you simply can't put together an effective advertisement, email, sales letter, or website by stringing together random phrases from this book willy-nilly. First, you have to do your homework, your research. Because although the words and phrases in this book can help you write more powerful and polished copy, first you must gather facts, both about the product you are selling and the market you are selling it to.

Digital and print copy persuades readers, in part, by giving them useful information about the products being advertised. The more facts you include in your copy, the better.

When you have a file full of facts at your fingertips, writing good copy is easy. You simply select the most relevant facts and describe them in a clear, concise, direct fashion.

But when copywriters don't bother to dig for facts, they fall back on fancy phrases and puffed-up expressions to fill the empty space on the page. The words sound nice, but they don't sell because the copy doesn't inform.

Here's a four-step procedure I use to get the information I need to write persuasive, fact-filled copy for my clients. This technique should be helpful to copywriters, account executives, and ad managers alike.

Step #1: Get all previously published material on the product.

For an existing product, there's a mountain of literature you can send to the copywriter as background information. This material includes:

- Tear sheets of previous ads
- Brochures
- Catalogs
- Article reprints
- Technical papers
- Copies of speeches
- Audiovisual scripts
- Press kits
- Swipe files of competitors' ads and literature.
- Emails
- E-newsletters
- White papers
- Webpages

Did I hear someone say they can't send me this material because their product is new? Nonsense. The birth of every new product is accompanied by mounds of paperwork you can give the copywriter. These materials include:

- Internal memos
- Letters of technical information

- Product specifications
- Engineering drawings
- Business and marketing plans
- Reports
- Proposals
- Prototypes

By studying this material, the copywriter should have 80 percent of the information he needs to write the copy. And he can get the other 20 percent by picking up the phone and asking questions. Steps #2–4 outline the questions he should ask about the product, the audience, and the objective of the copy.

Step #2: Ask Questions About the Product.

- What are its features and benefits? (Make a complete list.)
- Which benefit is the most important?
- How is the product different from the competition's? (Which features are exclusive? Which are better than the competition's?)
- If the product isn't different, which attributes can be stressed that haven't been stressed by the competition?
- Which technologies does the product compete against?
- What are the applications of the product?
- Which industries can use the product?
- Which problems does the product solve in the marketplace?
- How is the product positioned in the marketplace?
- How does the product work?
- How reliable is the product?
- How efficient?
- How economical?
- Who has bought the product, and what do they say about it?
- Which materials, sizes, and models is it available in?

- How quickly does the manufacturer deliver the product?
- What kind of service and support does the manufacturer offer?
- Is the product guaranteed?

Step #3: Ask Questions About Your Audience.

- Who will buy the product? (What markets is it sold to?)
- What is the customer's main concern? (Price, delivery, performance, reliability, service maintenance, quality efficiency?)
- What is the character of the buyer?
- What motivates the buyer?
- How many different buying influences must the copy appeal to? Two tips on getting to know your audience:
    - If you are writing an ad, read issues of the magazine in which the ad will appear.
    - If you are writing direct mail, find out which mailing lists will be used and study the list descriptions.

Step #4: Determine the Objective of Your Copy.

This objective may be one or more of the following:

- To generate inquiries
- To generate sales
- To answer inquiries
- To qualify prospects
- To transmit product information
- To build brand recognition and preference
- To build company image
- To build a list
- To boost open rates

- To increase click-through rates
- To increase conversion rates
- To upsell
- To cross-sell
- To generate bigger average order size
- To generate more frequent purchases

Before you write copy, study the product—its features, benefits, past performance, applications, and markets. Digging for the facts will pay off, because in business-to-business advertising, specifics sell.

Appendix II:
The Eight Fundamental Steps of Persuasive Writing

What are the characteristics that make copy effective? Why does one ad make a lasting impression and sell merchandise, while another falls flat and doesn't generate enough revenue to pay its own cost?

Virtually all persuasive copy contains the eight elements described in this article. The successful promotion:

1. Gains attention
2. Focuses on the customer
3. Stresses benefits
4. Differentiates you from the competition
5. Proves its case
6. Establishes credibility
7. Builds value
8. Closes with a call to action

All ads do not have all eight characteristics in equal proportions. Depending on the product, some of these elements will be dominant in your ad; others subordinate.

Let's take telephone service as an example. If you are AT&T, MCI, or Sprint, you have a long track record of success and a well-established reputation. Therefore, you will be naturally strong in elements five and six (proving your case and establishing your credibility).

A new telephone services provider, on the other hand, does not have a track record or reputation; therefore, these two elements will not be the dominant themes in the copy. Instead, the strongest element might be number three (benefits the service offers customers) or perhaps number four (differentiation in service resulting from superior technology).

Each product or service has natural strengths and weaknesses. The strengths are emphasized and the weaknesses deemphasized. But all eight elements must be present to some degree, or the ad won't work.

Here are the eight elements of persuasion discussed in a bit more detail, with examples of how to achieve each in your copy:

Element #1: Gain Attention.

If an ad fails to gain attention, it fails totally. Unless you gain the prospect's attention, he or she won't read any of your copy. And if the prospect doesn't read your copy, he or she won't receive the persuasive message you've so carefully crafted.

There are numerous ways to gain attention. Sex certainly is one of them. Look at the number of products—abdominal exercises, health clubs, cars, Club Med, clothes, beer, soft drinks, chewing gum—that feature attractive bodies in their ads and commercials. It may be sexist or base, but it works.

Similarly, you can use visuals to get prospects to pay attention. Parents (and almost everyone else) are attracted to pictures of babies and young children. Puppies and kittens also strike a chord in our hearts. Appealing visuals can get your ad noticed.

Since so much advertising is vague and general, being specific in your copy sets it apart from other ads and creates interest. A letter promoting collection services to dental practices begins as follows:

"How we collected over $20 million
in unpaid bills over the past two years
for thousands of dentists nationwide"

Dear Dentist:
It's true.

In the past two years alone, IC Systems has collected more than $20 million in outstanding debt for dental practices nationwide.

That's $20 million these dentists might not otherwise have seen if they had not hired IC Systems to collect their past due bills for them.

What gains your attention is the specific figure of $20 million dollars. Every collection agency promises to collect money. But saying that you have gotten $20 million in results is specific, credible, and memorable.

Featuring an offer that is free, low in price, or unusually attractive is also an effective attention-getter. A full-page newspaper ad from Guaranteed Term Life Insurance announces, "NOW . . . $1 a week buys Guaranteed Term Life Insurance for New Yorkers over 50." Not only does the $1 offer draw you in, but the headline also gains attention by targeting a specific group of buyers (New Yorkers over 50).

You know that in public speaking, you can gain attention by shouting or talking loudly. This direct approach can work in copy, especially in retail advertising. An ad for Lord & Taylor department store proclaims in large, bold type: STARTS TODAY . . . ADDITIONAL 40% OFF WINTER FASHIONS." Not clever or fancy, but of interest to shoppers looking to save money.

Another method of engaging the prospect's attention is to ask a provocative question. *Bits & Pieces*, a management magazine, begins its subscription mailing with this headline. "What do Japanese managers have that American managers sometimes lack?" Don't you want to at least read the next sentence to find the answer?

A mailing for a book club has this headline on the outer envelope:
Why is the McGraw-Hill Chemical Engineers' Book Club
giving away—practically for FREE—this special 50th
Anniversary Edition of *Perry's Chemical Engineers' Handbook?*

To chemical engineers, who know that Perry's costs about $125 per copy, the fact that someone would give it away is indeed a curiosity—and engineers, being curious people, want to get the answer.

Injecting news into copy, or announcing something that is new or improved, is also a proven technique for getting attention. A mailing offering subscriptions to a health newsletter had this headline:

"Here Are Astonishing Nutritional Therapies and Alternative Treatments You'll *Never* Hear About From the Medical Establishment, the FDA, Drug Companies or Even Your Doctor . . . " *Three decades of medical research breakthroughs from the Atkins Center for Complementary Medicine . . . revealed at last!*

The traditional Madison Avenue approach to copy—subtle word play and cleverness—often fails to get attention because many people reading the ad either don't get it, or if they do get it, they don't think it's that funny (or they think it's funny, but that doesn't compel them to read the ad or buy the product). A newspaper ad for a New Jersey hospital, promoting its facilities for treating kidney stones without surgery (ultrasonic sound waves are used to painlessly break up and dissolve the stone), carried this headline:

The End of the Stone Age.

Clever? Yes. But as former kidney stone patients, we can tell you that having kidney stones is not a fun, playful subject, and this headline misses the mark. The kidney stone sufferer wants to know he can go to his local hospital, get fast treatment, avoid an operation and a hospital stay, have the procedure be painless, and get rid of the kidney stones that are causing his current discomfort. Therefore, the headline "Get Rid of Painless Kidney Stones—Without Surgery," while less clever, is more direct and works better with this topic and this audience.

Element #2: Focus on the Customer.

When writing copy, start with the prospect, not with the product. Your prospects are interested primarily in themselves—their goals, their problems, their needs, their hopes, their fears, their dreams and aspirations. Your product or service is of secondary importance, the degree of concern being determined by the potential for the product or service to address one of the prospect's wants or needs, or solve one of their problems.

Effective copy speaks directly to a specific audience and identifies their preferences, quirks, behavior, attitudes, needs, or requirements. A recruitment brochure for a computer consultant firm, for example, has this headline on the cover:

> Introducing a unique career opportunity only a few dozen computer professionals in the country will be able to take advantage of this year . . .

The headline is effective, because it focuses on the prospects (Information Systems professionals) and one of their main concerns in life (their career), rather than the consulting firm and its history, as most such brochures do.

Write from the customer's point of view—e.g., not "Introducing our Guarda-Health Employee Benefit Program," but "At last you can combat the huge health insurance premiums threatening to put your small business *out* of business."

WEKA Publishing, in a direct mail package promoting the Electronics Repair Manual, a do-it-yourself guide for hobbyists and others who want to repair their own home and office electronics, uses copy that speaks directly to the personality type of the potential buyer:

> If you're handy . . . fascinated by electronics and the world of high-tech . . . are happiest with a tool in your hand . . . and respond to household problems and broken appliances with a defiant "I'll do it myself" . . .

. . . then fun, excitement, the thrill of discovery, time and money saved, and the satisfaction of a job well done await you when you preview our newly updated *Electronics Repair Manual* at no risk for a full thirty days.

A good way to ensure that you are focusing on the prospects, and not yourself or your product or your company, is to address the prospect directly in the copy as "you." For example:

Dear Health Care Administrator:

You know how tough it is to make a decent profit margin in today's world of managed care . . . and how the HMOs and other plans are putting even more of a squeeze on your margins to fill their own already-swelling coffers.

But what you may not be aware of is the techniques health care providers nationwide are using to *fight back* . . . and get paid every dollar they deserve for the important work they do.

This direct mail copy, which successfully launched a new publication, works because it focuses on the prospects and their problems (making money from their health care business), and not on the publication, its editors, or its features or columns.

Copy that fails to focus on the prospect often does so because the copywriter does not understand the prospect. If you are writing to metal shop managers, attend a metalworking trade show, read a few issues of the trade publications they subscribe to and interview some of these prospects in person or over the phone. Study focus group transcripts, attend live focus group sessions, or even accompany salespeople on sales calls to these prospects. The better you understand your target audience, the more you have a feel for the way they think and what they think about and the more effectively you can target copy that speaks to those concerns.

Element #3: Stress Benefits.

Although, depending on your audience, your prospects may be interested both in the features and the benefits of your product or service, it is almost never sufficient to discuss features only.

Virtually all successful copy discusses benefits. Copy aimed at a lay audience would primarily stress benefits, mentioning features mainly to convince the prospects that the product can in fact deliver the benefits promised in the ad.

Copy aimed at specialists often gives equal play to features and benefits, or may even primarily stress features. But whenever a feature is described, it must be linked to a customer benefit it provides. Buyers not only want to know what the product is and what it does, but they want to know how it can help them achieve the benefits they want—such as saving money, saving time, making money, being happier, looking better, or feeling fitter.

In copy for technical products, clearly explaining the feature makes the benefit more believable. Don't just say a product has greater capacity; explain which feature of the product allows it to deliver this increased capacity. A brochure for Lucent Technologies wireless CDMA technology explains, "CDMA gives you up to 10 times the capacity of analog cellular with more efficient use of spectrum. Use of a wideband block of radio frequency (RF) spectrum for transmission (1.25 MHz) enables CDMA to support up to 60 or more simultaneous conversations on a given frequency allocation."

A brochure for a computer consulting firm tells corporate IT managers how working with outside consultants can be more cost-effective than hiring staff, thus saving money:

> When you augment your IT department with our staff consultants, you pay our staff consultants only when they work for you. If the need ends tomorrow, so does the billing. In addition, various studies estimate the cost of hiring a new staff member at 30 to 60 percent or more of the annual salary (an executive search

firm's fee alone can be 30 percent of the base pay). These expenditures are 100% eliminated when you staff through EJR.

In an ad for a software package that creates a letterhead using a PC and a laser printer, the copy stresses the benefits of ease, convenience, and cost savings vs. having to order stationery from a printer:

Now save thousands of dollars on stationery printing costs
Every day, law firms struggle with the expense and inconvenience of engraved and preprinted stationery.

Now, in a sweeping trend to cut costs without sacrificing prestige, many are trading in their engraved letterhead for Instant Stationery desktop software from Design Forward Technologies.

With Instant Stationery, you can laser-print your WordPerfect documents and letterhead together on whatever grade of blank bond paper you choose. Envelopes, too. Which means you never have to suffer the cost of expensive preprinted letterhead—or the inconvenience of loading stationery into your desktop printer—ever again.

Element #4: Differentiate Yourself From the Competition.

Today, your customer has more products and services to choose from than ever. For example, a customer walking into a supermarket can choose from more than XX different brands of cereal, XX different brands of shampoo, and XX different flavors and brands of soft drink.

Therefore, to make our product stand out in the buyer's mind, and convince him or her that it is better and different than the competition, you must differentiate it from those other products in your copy. Crispix cereal, for example, was advertised as the cereal that "stays crisp in milk." Post Raisin Bran was advertised as the only raisin bran having "two scoops of raisins" in each box of cereal. A cookie maker recently ran a campaign promoting "100 chips" in every bag of chocolate chip cookies.

Companies that make a commodity product often differentiate themselves on the basis of service, expertise, or some other intangible. BOC Gases, for example, promotes itself as a superior vendor not because their product is better (they sell oxygen, and one oxygen molecule is basically the same as another), but in their ability to use oxygen and technology to benefit the customer's business. Here is copy from a brochure aimed at steelmakers:

> An oxygen supplier who knows oxygen *and* EAF steelmaking can be the strategic partner who gives you a sustainable competitive advantage in today's metals markets. And that's where BOC Gases can help.

If your product is unique within its market niche, stress this in your copy. For example, there are dozens of stock market newsletters. But IPO Insider claims to be the only IPO bulletin aimed at the consumer (there are other IPO information services, but these target professional investors and money managers). In their subscription promotion, the IPO Insider says:

> IPO Insider is the *only* independent research and analysis service in the country designed to help the individual investor generate greater-than-average stock market profits in select recommended IPOs.

Lucent Technologies, the AT&T spin-off, competes with many other companies that manufacture telecommunications network equipment. They differentiate themselves by stressing the tested reliability of their switch, which has been documented as superior to other switches in the industry. One brochure explains:

> The 5ESS-2000 Switch is one of the most reliable digital switches available for wireless systems today. According to the U.S. Federal Communication Commission's (FCC) ARMIS report,

the 5ESS-2000 switch has the least down-time of any switch used in U.S. networks, exceeding Bellcore's reliability standards by 200%. With an installed base of more than 2,300 switches, the 5ESS-2000 Switch currently serves over 72 million lines in 49 countries.

Element #5: Prove your Case.

Element #4, just discussed, claims product differentiation. Element #3 claims substantial benefits to product purchasers. The reason why these elements cannot stand alone is precisely that they are claims—claims made in a paid advertisement, by the advertiser. Therefore, skeptical consumers do not usually accept them at face value. If you say you are better, faster, or cheaper, and you do not back up your claims with proof, people won't believe you.

ICS convinces dentists it is qualified to handle their collections by presenting facts and statistics as follows:

> The nationwide leader in dental-practice collections, IC Systems has collected past due accounts receivables for 45,717 dental practices since 1963. Over 20 state dental associations recommend our services to their members.
>
> *IC Systems can collect more of the money your patients owe you.* Our overall recovery rate for dental collections is 12.4% higher than the American Collectors' Association national average of 33.63%. (For many dental practices, we have achieved recovery rates even higher!)

BOC Gases tells customers that the gas mixtures they sell in cylinders are accurately blended, and therefore that the composition listed on the label is what the buyer will find inside the container. They make this argument credible by explaining their blending and weighing methodology:

Each mixture component is weighed into the cylinder on a high-capacity, high-sensitivity equal-arm balance having a typical precision of +10 mg at 95 percent confidence. Balance accuracy is confirmed prior to weighing by calibration with NIST-traceable Class S weights. Electronic integration of the precision balance with an automated filling system provides extremely accurate mixtures with tight blend tolerances.

Many stock market newsletters promise big winners that will make the reader rich if he or she subscribes. Since everyone says it, the statement is usually greeted with skepticism. The newsletter Gold Stocks Advisory combats this skepticism by putting their recent successes right on the outer envelope and at the top of page one of their sales letter:

A sample of Paul Sarnoff's recent high-profit gold stock picks:

Company:	Purchase Price:	Year High:	% Increase/Time frame:	Potential profit on 10,000 shares:
Gold Canyon	C70 cents	C$10.50	2793% in 14 months	C$195,500
Coral Gold	C$1.20	C$6.45	438% in 8 months	C$52,500
Bema Gold	C$2.20	C$13.05	439 in 20 months	C$108,500
Jordex	C70 cents	C$3.75	435% in 6 months	C$26,300
Glamis Gold	US$1	US$8.88	788% in 84 months	US$78,800
Barrick Gold	US$4.81	US$32.88	584% in 96 months	$280,700

The most powerful tool for proving your case is to demonstrate a good track record in your field, showing that your product or service is successful in delivering the benefits and other results you promise. One way to create the perception of a favorable track record is to include case histories and success stories in your copy. Testimonials from satisfied customers are another technique for convincing prospects that you can do what you say you can do. You can also impress prospects by showing them a full or partial list of your customers.

Share with readers any results your firm has achieved for an individual customer or group of customers. IC Systems, for example, impressed dentists by telling them that the company has collected $20 million in past due bills over the past two years alone—a number that creates the perception of a service that works.

Element #6: Establish Credibility.

In addition to the benefits you offer, the products and services you deliver that offer these benefits, and the results you have achieved, prospective buyers will ask the question, "Who are you?"

In terms of persuasion, of the three major topics you discuss in your ad—the prospect, the product, and the product vendor—the "corporate" story is usually the least important. The prospect is primarily interested in himself and his problems and needs and interested in your product or service only as a means of solving those problems or filling those needs. The prospect is interested in your company only as it relates to your ability to reliably make, deliver, install, and service the product he buys from you.

Yet the source of the product or service—the company—still is a factor in influencing purchase decisions. In the early days of personal computing, IBM was the preferred brand—not because IBM necessarily made a superior computer at a better price, but because if something went wrong, IBM could be counted on for fast, reliable, effective service and support. As PCs became more of a commodity and local computer resellers and stores offered better service, the service and support reputation of IBM became less of an advantage, and their PC sales declined.

Here are some examples of copy in which the vendor gives credentials designed to make the consumer feel more comfortable in doing business with them and choosing them over other suppliers advertising similar products and services:

We guarantee the best technical service and support. I was a compressor service technician at Ingersoll Rand, and in the last 20 years have personally serviced more than 250 compressors at over 80 companies.

For nearly 100 years, BOC Gases has provided innovative gas technology solutions to meet process and production needs. We have supplied more than 20,000 different gases and gas mixtures—in purities up to 99.99999 percent—to 2 million customers worldwide.

Lion Technology is different. For nearly two decades, we have dedicated ourselves 100% to training managers, engineers, and others in environmental compliance-related subjects. Since 1989, our firm has conducted more than 1,400 workshops nationwide on these topics.

You'll find some of Paul's fundamental research in precious metals summed up in his more than 60 best-selling books including *Silver Bulls* and *Trading with Gold*. Paul's unique blending of solid research, combined with an unprecedented record of success in picking gold stocks, may have been what moved one New York Times reporter to dub him "the dean of commodities researchers."

Credentials you can list in your copy include year founded, number of years in business, number of employees, annual revenues, number of locations, number of units sold, patents and product innovations, awards, commendations, publications, membership and participation in professional societies, seals of approval, agency ratings, independent survey results, media coverage, number of customers, and in-house resources (financial, technological, and human).

Element #7: Build Value.

It's not enough to convince prospects you have a great product or a superior service. You must also show them that the value of your offer far exceeds the price you are asking for it. You may have the best widget in the $100 to $200 price range of medium-size widgets, but why should the prospect pay $200 for your widget when they can get another brand for half the price? One argument might be lower total cost of ownership. Although your widget costs more to buy, its greater reliability and performance save and make your firm money, which, over the long haul, far exceeds the difference in price between you and brand X.

Stress cost of ownership vs. cost of purchase. The purchase price is not the only cost of owning something. There is the cost of maintenance, support, repair, refurbishment, operation, and, when something wears out, replacement. Therefore, the product that costs the least to buy may not actually cost the least to own; oftentimes, it is the most expensive to own!

Example: Several companies are now selling artificial bone substitutes for orthopedic surgeons to use in bone graft operations. As of this writing, a small container of the artificial bone substitute, containing enough material for one spine surgery, can cost $500 to $800.

The shortsighted buyer sees this as expensive, especially since bone graft can be taken from other sites in the patient's own body, and there is no cost for this material.

But is there really no cost? Collecting bone graft from the patient's own body adds about an hour to the surgical procedure. With operating room time at about $1,000 an hour, it makes sense to pay $750 for bone material and eliminate this extra hour in the OR.

That's not all. Often removing the bone from a donor site causes problems that can result in an extra day's stay in the hospital. That's another $1,000 down the tubes. And the removal of bone from the donor site can cause infection, which must be treated with costly antibiotics. Also, the removal process can cause pain; how do you measure the cost of the patient's added suffering? So while $750 for a small vial of artificial bone may seem initially expensive, it is in fact a bargain when compared with the alternative (which, on the surface, appears to have zero cost).

Here's a simpler example. You need to buy a photocopier for your home office. Copier A costs $900. Copier B costs $1,200. The features are essentially the same, and the reputations of the brands are comparable. Both have an expected lifetime of 120,000 copies. Most people would say, "Everything's the same except price, so buy copier A and save $300." Copier A compares itself feature for feature with Copier B and runs an ad with the headline "Copier A vs. Our Competition . . . We Can Do Everything They Can Do . . . at 25% Off the Price."

But you are the copywriter for the makers of Copier B. You ask them what it costs to make a copy. Their cost per copy is 2 cents. You investigate Copier A and find out that the toner cartridges are more expensive, so that the cost per copy is 4 cents. You can now advertise copies at "half the cost of our competitor."

What's more, a simple calculation shows that if Copier B is 2 cents a copy cheaper, and you use the machine to make 120,000 copies, your savings over the life of the machine is $2,400. Therefore, an investment in Copier B pays you pack eight times the extra $300 it cost to buy. This is additional ammunition you can use in your copier to establish that purchase price is not the ultimate factor determining buying decisions, and that Copier B offers a greater overall value to the buyer.

If your product costs slightly more up front but actually saves money in the long run, stress this in your sales talk. Everyone knows that the cheapest product is not automatically the best buy; corporate buyers are becoming especially concerned with this cost of ownership concept. Only government business, which is awarded based on sealed proposals and bids, seems to still focus solely on the lowest price. And even that is slowly changing.

The key to establishing value is to convince the prospects that the price you ask is "a drop in the bucket" compared with the money your product will make or save them, or the other benefits it delivers. Some examples:

What would you do if the EPA assessed a $685,000 fine against your company for noncompliance with environmental regulations you *weren't even aware existed*?

Now get the special 50th Anniversary Edition of
Perrys Chemical Engineers' Handbook . . .
. . . for only $4.97 (list price: $129.50)
with your No-Risk Trial Membership in McGraw-Hill's
Chemical Engineers' Book Club.

Another way to establish value is to compare the cost of your product with more expensive products or services that address the same basic need:

The cost of The Novell Companion, including the 800+ page reference binder and NetWare utilities on diskette, is normally $89 plus $6.50 for shipping and handling. This is *less* than a NetWare consultant would charge to advise you for just one hour . . . yet The Novell Companion is there to help you administer and manage your network, year after year.

If your product or service is used over a period of time, as most are, you can reduce the "sticker shock" that comes with quoting a high up-front price by showing the cost over the extended usage period. For instance, a life insurance policy with an annual premium of $200 "gives your loved ones protection for just 55 cents a day." The latter seems more affordable, although the two prices are equivalent.

Element #8: Close with a Call to Action.

Copy is written to bring about a change—that is, to cause prospects to change their opinion, attitude, beliefs, purchasing plans, brand preferences, or immediate buying actions.

To effect this change, your copy must be specific about the action the prospect should take if they are interested in what you've said and how to take advantage of your offer or at least find out more. Tell them to clip and mail the coupon, call the toll free phone number, visit your website, come to your store, request a free estimate, or whatever. Specify the next step directly in your copy, or else few people will take it. Some examples:

> When you call, be sure to ask how you can get a FREE copy of our new audiocassette, *"How to Get Better Results From Your Collection Efforts."* In just seven minutes listening time, you'll discover at least half a dozen of the techniques IC Systems uses—and you can use, too—to get more people to pay what they owe you.
>
> For a complimentary copy of the *Secrets of Building a World-Class Website* audiocassette, complete and mail the survey enclosed or fax it today to 1 888 FAX 2IBM (1 888 329 2426).
>
> *Put BOC's quality gas solutions to work in your plant—starting today.*
>
> Think it's time to talk with a gas supplier that really knows your business and has real solutions to your problems? Call your BOC Gases representative today. Or visit our website at http:// www.boc.com.

Appendix III: Copyediting Checklist

- Is the copy clear? Have you said everything as clearly and simply as possible?
- Have you used the simplest words? Always prefer simple words to complex words, small words to big words.
- Is the opening paragraph brief? It should never take more than three lines of copy.
- Are sentences and paragraphs too long? Look for opportunities to break long paragraphs and sentences into shorter ones.
- Can you break the text into separate sections? Subheads are useful for organizing long copy into bite-sized, easy-to-digest chunks of text.
- Do the subheads sell? Subheads should be more than descriptive labels; they should communicate key product benefits. The reader should be able to get the gist of your sales pitch just by skimming the subheads of your ad.
- Is the headline as strong as it can be? Does it grab attention, deliver a message, select the audience, and lure the reader into the body copy?
- Does the organization make sense? Does the ad tell a cohesive sales story? Are sales points logically organized in order of importance or according to the sequence the buyer goes through in making a purchase decision?
- Does the copy flow smoothly? Eliminate awkward transitions. Make sure the copy flows smoothly from point

to point. If you have trouble with this, you might simply list your sales points and number them consecutively.

- Is the copy concise? Tighten wherever possible by editing out all unnecessary words, phrases, and sentences.
- Is the ad complete? Does it contain all necessary information? Have you told the whole story?
- Is it persuasive? If you were the prospect, would this ad persuade you to buy the product? If not, why not?
- Is the copy believable? Will it overcome the reader's doubts, fears, and hesitation? If not, what facts or arguments can be added to correct this problem? Can testimonials be used to strengthen your case?
- Will the reader find the copy interesting? The question is not whether you or other people in your company like or dislike the ad; it's whether the ad can hold the attention of the logical prospect for your product. Your prospect will find the ad interesting if it's relevant and offers benefits he wants to have.
- Is the ad prospect-centered? Is the ad built around the needs, concerns, and desires of your prospect?
- Does the copy talk to the prospect, person-to-person? The tone should be warm, friendly, conversational, natural, and helpful—like one friend talking to another. Don't be afraid to use personal pronouns and address the reader directly as "you."
- Is the tone of the copy enthusiastic? A good salesperson is enthusiastic about his product. This enthusiasm should come across in your copy.
- Can the copy be written with a little more flair? If you see an opportunity to say something in a clever way that will enhance your message (vs. cleverness for the sake of being clever), take it. But don't force cleverness. And don't clown around. Sincerity and a straightforward manner are much better salesmen than the so-called "creative" approach embraced on Madison Avenue.

Appendix IV: The Unique Selling Proposition

In 1961, Rosser Reeves published his classic book *Reality in Advertising* in which he introduced the notion of the Unique Selling Proposition, or USP.

Today, the book is out of print and difficult to get. As a result, most practicing direct marketers don't know the original definition of a USP. Their lack of knowledge often produces USPs that are weak and ineffective.

According to Reeves, there are three requirements for a USP (and I am quoting, in the italics, from *Reality in Advertising* directly):

1. Each advertisement must make a proposition to the consumer. Each must say, "Buy this product, and you will get this specific benefit."

Your headline must contain a benefit—a promise to the reader.

2. The proposition must be one that the competition either cannot, or does not, offer.

Here's where the "unique" in Unique Selling Proposition comes in. It is not enough merely to offer a benefit. You must also *differentiate* your product.

3. The proposition must be so strong that it can move the mass millions, i.e., pull over new customers to your product.

The differentiation cannot be trivial. It must be a difference that is very important to the reader.

Why do so many advertisements fail?

One reason is that the marketer has not formulated a strong USP for his product and built his advertising upon it.

Formulating a USP isn't difficult, but it does take some thinking; and many people don't like to think.

But when you start creating direct mail and advertising without first thinking about what your USP is, your marketing is weak because there is nothing in it to compel the reader to respond. It looks and sounds like everyone else, and what it says isn't important to the reader.

In general advertising for packaged goods, marketers achieve differentiation by building a strong brand at a cost of millions or even billions of dollars.

Coca Cola has an advantage because of its brand. If you want a cola, you can get it from a dozen soda makers. But if you want a Coke, you can only get it from Coca Cola.

Intel has achieved a similar brand dominance, at an extraordinary cost, with its Pentium line of semiconductors.

Most direct marketers are too small, and have too strong a need to generate an immediate positive ROI from their marketing, to engage in this kind of expensive brand building. So we use other means to achieve the differentiation in our USP.

One popular method is to differentiate your product or service from the competition based on a feature that your product or service has and they don't.

The common error here is building the USP around a feature that, while different, is unimportant to the prospect, and therefore unlikely to move him to try your product or service.

For example, in the pump industry, it is common for pump manufacturers to attempt to win customers by advertising a unique design feature. Unfortunately, these design twists often result in no real performance improvement, no real advantage that the customer cares about.

Realizing that they could not differentiate based on a concrete design principle, Blackmer pump took a different tack: to create a USP based upon *application* of the product.

Their trade ads showed a Yellow Pages ripped out of an industrial buying guide, full of listings for pump manufacturers, including Blackmer. Their company name was circled in pen.

The headline of the ad read, "There are only certain times you should call Blackmer for a pump. Know when?"

Body copy explained (and I am paraphrasing here), "In many applications, Blackmer performs no better or worse than any pumps, and so we are not a particularly advantageous choice."

But, the ad went on, for certain applications (viscous fluids, fluids containing abrasives, slurries, and a few other situations), Blackmer was proven to outperform all other pumps and were the logical brand of choice. Blackmer closed the ad by offering a free technical manual proving the claim.

My old friend, Jim Alexander, of Alexander Marketing in Grand Rapids, Michigan, created this campaign and tells me it worked extremely well.

The easiest situation in which to create a strong USP is when your product has a unique feature—one that competitors lack—that delivers a strong benefit.

This must be an advantage the customer really cares about. Not one that, though a difference, is trivial.

But what if such a proprietary advantage does not exist? What if your product is basically the same as the competition, with no special features?

Reeves has the answer here, too. He said the uniqueness can either stem from a strong brand or from "a claim not otherwise made in that particular form of advertising"—that is, other products may have this feature too, but advertisers haven't told consumers about it.

A brand example from packaged goods advertising: "M&Ms melt in your mouth, not in your hand." Once M&M established this claim as their USP, what could the competition do? Run an ad that said, "We *also* melt in your mouth, not in your hand!"?

In his book *Scientific Advertising*, Claude Hopkins gives an example of a USP that has become a classic story.

The short version: an ad man walking through his beer client's brewery was fascinated by a machine that blasted steam into beer bottles to sanitize them.

"Don't use that in advertising," the brewer told the ad man. "It is nothing unique; every brewer does the same."

"Maybe," the ad man replied, "but I had never heard of it before, and neither has any of the beer-drinking public."

He then created a successful ad campaign for a beer advertised as "so pure, the bottles are washed in live steam."

One more point: as marketers, we are compelled to create advertising that generates net revenues in excess of its cost. Reeves believed all advertising had to do this. He defined advertising as "the art of getting a USP into the heads of the most people at the lowest possible cost." If I were to modify his definition, I would change it to "getting a USP into the heads of the people *most likely to buy the product*, at the lowest possible advertising cost."

Appendix V:
The BDF Formula

How well do you really know your customers? Reading the list data cards is a good way to find out something about the folks you are mailing to, but it's not enough. Knowing that you are writing to farmers, Information Technology (IT) professionals, or plumbers is just the start. You have to dig deeper. But how?

To write powerful copy, you have to go beyond the demographics to understand what really motivates these people—who they are, what they want, how they feel, and what their biggest problems and concerns are that your product can help solve.

One direct marketer told me, "We want to reach prospects on three levels—intellectual, emotional, and personal."

Intellectual is the first level and, while effective, not as strong as the other two. An intellectual appeal is based on logic—e.g., "Buy the stocks we recommend in our investment newsletter, and you will beat the market by 50 to 100 percent."

More powerful is to reach the prospect on an *emotional* level. Emotions that can be tapped include fear, greed, love, vanity, and, for fundraising, benevolence. Going back to our example of a stock market newsletter, the emotional appeal might be "Our advice can help you cut your losses and make much more money, so you become much wealthier than your friends and neighbors. You'll be able to pay cash for your next car—a Lexus, BMW, or any luxury automobile you care to own—and you'll sleep better at night."

The most powerfully you can reach people is on a *personal* level. Again, from our example of a stock market newsletter: "Did you lose a small fortune in the April 2000 tech stock meltdown? So much that it put your dreams of retirement or financial independence on hold? Now you can gain back everything you lost, rebuild your net worth, and make your dream of early retirement of financial independence come true. A lot sooner than you think."

To reach your prospects on all three levels—intellectual, emotional, and personal—you must understand what copywriter Michael Masterson calls the buyer's "Core Complex." These are the emotions, attitudes, and aspirations that drive them, as represented by the formula BDF—beliefs, feelings, and desires:

- *Beliefs.* What does your audience believe? What is their attitude toward your product and the problems or issues it addresses?
- *Desires.* What do they want? What are their goals? What change do they want in their lives that your product can help them achieve?
- *Feelings.* How do they feel? Are they confident and brash? Nervous and fearful? What do they feel about the major issues in their lives, businesses, or industries?

For instance, we did this exercise with IT people, for a company that gives seminars in communication and interpersonal skills for IT professionals. Here's what we came up with in a group meeting:

- *Beliefs.* IT people think they are smarter than other people, technology is the most important thing in the world, users are stupid, and management doesn't appreciate them enough.
- *Desires.* IT people want to be appreciated and recognized. They also prefer to deal with computers and avoid people whenever possible. And they want bigger budgets.
- *Feelings.* IT people often have an adversarial relationship with management and users, both of whom they service.

They feel others dislike them, look down upon them, and do not understand what they do.

Based on this analysis, particularly the feelings, the company created a direct mail letter that was its most successful ever to promote a seminar "Interpersonal Skills for IT Professionals." The rather unusual headline: "Important news for any IT professional who has ever felt like telling an end user, 'Go to hell.'"

Before writing copy, write out in narrative form the BDF of your target market. Share these with your team and come to an agreement on them. Then write copy based on the agreed BDF.

Occasionally, insights into the prospect's desires and concerns can be gleaned through formal market research. For instance, a copywriter working on a cooking oil account was reading a focus group transcript and came across this comment from a user: "I fried chicken in the oil and then poured the oil back into a measuring cup. All the oil was there except one teaspoon."

This comment, buried in the appendix of a focus group report, became the basis of a successful TV campaign dramatizing the selling point that food did not absorb the oil and therefore was not greasy when cooked in it.

Veteran ad man Joe Sacco once had an assignment to write a campaign for a new needle used by diabetics to inject insulin. What was the key selling point?

The diabetics Sacco talked to all praised the needle because it was sharp. A nonuser would probably view being sharp as a negative. But if you have ever given yourself or anyone else an injection, you know that sharper needles go in smoother, with no pain. And Sacco wrote a successful ad campaign based on the claim that these needles were sharp, therefore enabling easier, pain-free insulin injection.

Copywriter Don Hauptman advises, "Start with the prospect, not the product." With BDF, you can quickly gain a deeper understanding of your prospects before you attempt to sell them something. Stronger marketing campaigns usually follow.

Appendix VI:
The Secret of the 4 U's

When prospects get your marketing message, they make a quick decision, usually in a couple of seconds, to open or delete it based largely on the subject line. But given the glut of promotional email today, how can you convince a busy prospect—in just a few words—that your message is worthy of attention?

The "4 U's" copywriting formula—which stands for urgent, unique, ultraspecific, and useful—can help.

Originally developed by my colleague Michael Masterson for writing more powerful headlines, the 4 U's formula works with articles, blog posts, websites, email subject lines, and more. I'll share it with you now.

According to this formula, strong subject lines are:

Urgent. Urgency gives the reader a reason to act now instead of later. You can create a sense of urgency in your subject line by incorporating a time element. For instance, "Make $100,000 working from home this year" has a greater sense of urgency than "Make $100,000 working from home." A sense of urgency can also be created with a time-limited special offer, such as a discount or premium if you order by a certain date.

Unique. The powerful subject line either says something new or, if it says something the reader has heard before, says it in a new and fresh way. For example, "Why Japanese women have beautiful skin" was the subject line in an email promoting a Japanese bath kit. This is different than the typical "Save 10 percent on Japanese Bath Kits."

Ultraspecific. Boardroom is the absolute master of ultraspecific bullets, known as "fascinations," that tease the reader into reading further and ordering the product. Examples: "What never to eat on an airplane,"

"Bills it's okay to pay late," and "Best time to file for a tax refund." They use such fascinations in direct mail as envelope teasers and in email as subject lines.

Useful. The strong subject line appeals to the reader's self-interest by offering a benefit. In the subject line "An Invitation to Ski & Save," the benefit is saving money.

When you have written your subject line, ask yourself how strong it is in each of these 4 U's. Use a scale of 1 to 4 (1 = weak, 4 = strong) to rank it in each category.

Rarely will a subject line rate a 3 or 4 on all four U's. But if your subject line doesn't rate a 3 or 4 on at least *three* of the U's, it's probably not as strong as it could be—and can benefit from some rewriting.

A common mistake is to defend a weak subject line by pointing to a good response. A better way to think is as follows: if the email generated a profitable response despite a weak subject line, imagine how much more money you could have made by applying the 4 U's.

A software marketer wrote to tell me he had sent out a successful email marketing campaign with the subject line "Free White Paper." How does this stack up against the 4 U's?

Urgent. There is no urgency or sense of timeliness. On a scale of 1 to 4, with 4 being the highest rating, "Free White Paper" is a 1.

Unique. Not every software marketer offers a free white paper, but a lot of them do. So "Free White Paper" rates only a 2 in terms of uniqueness.

Ultraspecific. Could the marketer have been less specific than "Free White Paper"? Yes, he could have just said, "Free bonus gift." So we rate "Free White Paper" a 2 instead of a 1.

Useful. I suppose the reader is smart enough to figure the white paper contains some helpful information he can use. On the other hand, the usefulness is in the specific information contained in the paper, which isn't even hinted at in the headline. And does the recipient, who already has too much to read, really need yet another "Free White Paper"? I rate it a 2. Specifying the topic would help, e.g., "Free White Paper shows how to cut training costs up to 90 percent with e-learning."

I urge you to go through this exercise with every email subject line you write. You can also apply the formula to other copy, both online and offline, including direct mail envelope teasers, ad headlines, letter leads, webpage headlines, subheads, and bullets.

Rate the line you've written in all four U's. Then rewrite it so you can upgrade your rating on at least 2 and preferably 3 or 4 of the categories by at least 1. This simple exercise may increase readership and response rates substantially for very little effort.

Appendix VII: Writing Copy: Where Do You Start?

A couple of my copywriting colleagues from Germany came to visit me in my office, and as we were chatting, the question came up: "When you sit down to write a promotion, where do you start?"

While there is no right answer—you should do whatever works for you—an informal survey of copywriters reveals that these are the most common starting points:

1. Headline. Many copywriters start with the headline. They write many different headlines. And then agonize over which one is best.

James Web Young recalls sitting at home one evening when the thought "Why does every man hope his first child will be a boy?" just popped into his head. He wrote it down and later used it as the headline for a successful ad.

Other copywriters just write a rough headline as a placeholder and write the entire promotion. Often, something they write in the body copy makes a stronger headline than their placeholder.

I prefer to get a strong headline (with subhead) down on the screen before I start writing the rest of the piece. Reason: the headline is your most articulate expression of the big selling idea behind your package, and if you can write a strong headline on it, you probably understand that big idea pretty well. The words and phrases in this book are there to give you an edge in writing stronger headlines.

2. A theme or big idea. Porter Stansberry and his team of copywriters, led by Mike Palmer, write virtually all of their promotions around a big idea, theme, or story. I believe they actually build products (in their case, newsletters) around big ideas they think will work in the mail.

One of the early promotions Porter wrote had the headline: "There's a new railroad across America." As I recall, the new railroad was a large fiber-optic data network. The big idea was that just as the railroads connected us in the early days of America, communications networks now connect us in modern times.

3. The prospect. Copywriter Don Hauptman says, "Start with the prospect, not the product." Another top copywriter, Sig Rosenblum, advises: "Don't talk about what's interesting to you. Talk about what's interesting to the prospect—his hopes, dreams, need, fears, problems, concerns, and desires."

Traditional advertising often centers on the product. Even Bill Bernbach's classic Volkswagen ad, "Think Small," focuses on the product, not the prospect—at least in the headline.

But a better approach is to start with what's on the prospect's mind— what he cares about—and then connect your product to the prospect's major need or problem.

4. The list. Ed McLean's classic letter for *Newsweek* began: "If the list upon which I found your name is any indication, this is not the first— nor will it be the last—subscription letter you receive. Quite frankly, your education and income set you apart from the general population and make you a highly rated prospect for everything from magazines to mutual funds."

Physician's Desk Reference, a directory of prescription drug data, beat a long-time control when they focused their mailings to specific lists. For instance, a mailing to a list of people who had bought their PDR three years earlier said, "Your PDR is now three years old and woefully out of date. Do not make prescribing or clinical decisions with PDR until you replace your dated edition with the new volume."

5. Core emotion. Superstar copywriter Clayton Makepeace says the most important thing to nail first when writing a promotion is a lead that somehow resonates with what he calls the prospect's "dominant resident emotion"—the strongest feeling he has relating to your product or the problem it solves.

Once he has a lead capturing that emotion, he writes a headline to get prospects to read it. Example: "LIES, LIES, LIES . . . we investors are fed up with everyone lying to us and wasting our money!"

6. The core buying complex. Michael Masterson, cofounder of AWAI, uses a similar approach, except that he starts with what he calls the "core buying complex." This consists of the beliefs, feelings, and desires the prospect has that relate to the product or offer.

A training firm launched a new seminar by making the title of the workshop the headline of the letter: "Interpersonal Skills for IT Professionals." It did not do well.

While analyzing the core buying complex, the marketing team determined that a key feeling of prospects—IT managers—was the adversarial nature of the relationship that often exists between IT professionals and end users.

They tested against the control a new letter with the headline: "Important news for any IT professional who has ever felt like telling an end user, 'Go to hell.'" The test pulled 6X more leads than the control.

7. A big problem. A great question to ask your client is "What's keeping your prospects up at night?" Then write a lead that acknowledges that problem.

My friend Sy Sperling became a multimillionaire by founding the Hair Club for Men. He began with tiny space ads in the *Daily News*.

These small space ads had no room for long headlines. If he wanted the headline in big, bold type, he only had room for a few words. His one-word headline focused on the biggest problem of men who had lost their hair: "BALD?"

8. *Body copy.* Write the body copy first. Then read it several times. Highlight any strong sentence or phrase you think should be moved closer to the front. One may be strong enough to move to the very front, as your headline.

Jim Reutz said in an interview he used a similar method to beat controls. He'd read the control until he found something buried in the middle that would make a strong headline and lead than the one the copywriter had used.

9. *The offer.* If the offer is extremely appealing, or your audience is one that responds to offer-driven promotions (e.g., book and record club buyers), you can start by writing the offer.

Years ago, the Chemical Engineer's Book Club introduced a new offer: join the club and get the major reference work in the field, *Perry's Chemical Handbook.*

The package I wrote worked very well. The outer envelope teaser was "Why are we giving away this new 50th anniversary edition of *Perry's Handbook* practically for FREE?"

10. *Order form.* An effective way to overcome writer's block, especially when writing longer documents, is to start with the easy parts. When writing a magalog, DM package, or landing page, that means for some copywriters starting with the order form.

To get something down on the screen, you can even copy the order form from the old promotion. Why not? Having that part done can energize you to move forward. And you can always come back to the order form and improve it later.

11. *Word file template.* Another way to overcome writer's block is to create a template for your new promotion in Word. Just copy the file from your last promotion, delete the text, and leave the outline: subheads and breaks indicating where the various elements go. Then start filling in the blank sections on the Word template.

12. Your swipe file. Keep a swipe file of controls in your market as well as strong mailings in other industries. Look to both files for ideas and inspiration when facing a blank screen on your new copywriting assignment. Copywriter Milt Pierce says: "A good swipe file is better than a college education."

Appendix VIII:
Ten Options for Illustrating
Your Promotions

1. Show a picture of the provider of the product. If you provide a service personally . . . or if your name is well linked with your company or product . . . you can be the star of your ad. Ads for Charles Schwab discount brokerage, for example, show a picture of Charles Schwab. Ads for Perdue chicken sometimes feature Frank Perdue. My high school friend, Gary Gerber, is now a successful eye doctor who appears weekly in his own newspaper ads. The power of this technique is that it builds people's trust in you and your company . . . since they can see the face behind the promise. So one possibility is to illustrate your ad with a picture of the person who provides the service or product.

2. Product as hero. In this approach, the ad is illustrated with a close-up photograph of the product against a plain background, which immediately gets the subject matter of the ad across to the reader. If you're selling sunglasses, show the glasses. If you're selling encyclopedias, show the encyclopedias.

A variation of this theme is to show a close-up photograph of the product in its package. This familiarizes the reader with your packaging, so when he goes to the store, he will notice it and reach for it on a supermarket shelf.

3. Show the product in use or the benefit of using the product. If you're advertising toothpaste, don't show toothpaste on a brush; show white teeth. If you're advertising a gas-fueled portable grill, show a happy family having a backyard barbecue.

4. Show the output of the product. If you're selling a pasta maker, don't show the machine; show a delicious plate of ready-to-eat linguini carbonara. If you're advertising a desktop publishing software package, don't show the software; show a beautifully designed computer-generated newsletter or report.

5. Before-and-after. An old standard, but still powerful. Example: For a hair replacement product, show before-and-after pictures that demonstrate how the product gave a bald man a full head of hair.

6. Diagram. In industrial, high-tech, or business product ads, consider using a diagram. Technical people respond well to visual information presented in the format to which they're accustomed. For instance: accountants like spreadsheets, computer programmers like flow charts or samples of programs, project managers like Gantt Charts, civil engineers like blueprints, and architects like architectural drawings.

7. Depict a lifestyle. This approach creates visual interest by allowing the reader to see himself in the ad, For example, an ad appealing to busy business executives might show an executive working late at night in his office, surrounded by a blizzard of paper, Ads for cigarettes, gourmet foods, and other "lifestyle" products often depict "yuppies" or other types of people the advertiser believes are the market for his product.

8. Testimonial. In a testimonial ad, where a customer is speaking in his own words about your product, show a picture of the customer for an added degree of credibility.

9. Scientific proof. Tables, charts, graphs, bar charts, pie charts, photographs.

10. All copy. In ads that are all copy and contain no visual, the headline becomes the visual focus. This is called either "editorial" or "native" advertising.

Appendix IX: How to Create Irresistible Offers

How important is the offer in marketing?

Answer: very. I have seen numerous tests in which a simple change of offer has increased the response rate by 25 percent to 900 percent—dramatically improving ROMD (return on marketing dollars) for the advertiser. The best of these winning b-to-b offers share six common characteristics . . . and to lift your response rates, your offers should, too.

Winning offers:

1—Are different or unique. The best offers are fresh and new. When copywriter Bill Jayme wrote the direct mail packaged that launched *New York* magazine, he proposed a sweepstakes. Sweepstakes have long been used to sell magazine subscriptions, but none has ever offered the prize Jayme dreamed up: dinner at Gracie Mansion with New York City's mayor.

Most investment newsletters offer free special reports as premiums. *The Sovereign Society*, a newsletter on offshore investing, offered something different: a free Swiss bank account—a gift not given by any other investment newsletter.

Most business magazines offer either discounted subscription rates or standard premiums like special reports, tote bags, or calculators. *Advertising Age* had a successful control where the premium was a ceramic coffee mug. Coffee mugs are nothing special. But this one was imprinted with a mock-up of an *Ad Age* cover. If the subscriber was Jan Smith, the headline on the mock issue of *Ad Age* was personalized to read: "Jan Smith Chosen as Marketing Genius of the Year."

2—Have a high degree of desirability. An unusual offer only works if it's something people really want.

A publisher was selling a loose-leaf service on how to manage Novell NetWare local area networks. Response rates doubled when a new direct mail promotion offered a disk with free software—a collection of utilities for Novell networks.

The 100 percent increase in orders confirmed that these software programs were tools network administrators obviously wanted to get their hands on. The outer envelope teaser read: "Yours FREE!—5 Powerful Programs to Help You Manage Your Novell NetWare Network More Efficiently and Easily—See Inside for Details on This Special Time-Limited Offer."

On the other hand, a financial newsletter mailed a renewal promotion that offered as a premium a pack of playing cards with the editor's picture on them. Not surprisingly, it flopped: who would want that?

3—Have a high perceived value, especially in relation to fulfillment cost. Free software has traditionally worked well as a premium. Software has a high perceived value in relation to the cost of goods. You know that purchased in a store or online, software packages can easily sell for $49 to $300 or more. Yet a CD with code on it can be duplicated for about a dollar.

But how much do you pay for a deck of playing cards at your local stationery store? About a dollar, right? Therefore, the perceived value of the playing cards given as a renewal promotion by the financial publisher mentioned earlier is only a dollar—hardly a financial motivator to renew a newsletter subscription that costs $79 a year.

In a promotion tied in with their sponsorship of the Olympics, IBM offered a special IBM Olympic pin as a premium. In reality, the item probably only cost and was worth a buck or so. But the mailer copy hinted that the item could become a collectible, creating an impression of potentially high value.

4—Dramatize the brand or USP. The Sovereign Society is a newsletter about offshore investing. The symbol for offshore investing has long been Swiss bank accounts. Therefore, the offer of a free Swiss bank account with a subscription to *The Sovereign Society* supports and dramatizes the newsletter's USP: making money and increasing privacy by investing offshore in things like Swiss bank accounts.

Even when the offer does not at first glance seem closely related to the product, a clever copywriter can find a connection. Example: years ago, *Newsweek* offered a free radio as a premium for new subscribers.

It would seem that, on the surface, a radio is a poor choice of premium: in the news area, radio and magazines compete with each other. But copywriter Milt Pierce used the differences between these media to make a logical connection between the premium and the product:

> Dear Reader:
> What's the fastest way to get the news?
>
> It's on the radio. That's why *Newsweek* wants you to have—as an introductory gift for new subscribers—this superb AM/FM radio.
>
> But what's the best way to get the news?
>
> You won't get just headlines and a rough outline of the news, with *Newsweek*, you'll get the news in depth . . .

5—Are easy to take advantage of. You should make it as easy and convenient as possible for the prospect to accept your offer.

How? To begin with, offer multiple response mechanisms: toll-free phone number . . . fax number . . . a hyperlink to a landing page (see www.thelandingpageguru.com) . . . email . . . even (gasp!) a postal address. Different prospects respond in different ways.

Create response mechanisms. In a direct mail package, enclose a fax-back form or business reply card (BRC) with your letter. If you want customers to enclose payment with their order, or privacy is a concern, also include a business reply envelope (BRE).

In a print ad, consider including a coupon or a bind-in BRC opposite the advertisement. On the web, landing pages should ask for the minimum information from the prospect when collecting leads. If you are building your opt-in e-list, ask for name and email address only. When you have multiple fields for the user to complete, use an asterisk (*) to indicate which are mandatory and make as many fields as possible optional. Conversion rates decline incrementally for each additional field you force the prospect to fill out.

The ease and convenience of accepting the offer can even be highlighted in the copy as a benefit. In a letter selling the *Board Report*, a newsletter for graphic designers, copywriter Sig Rosenblum makes a benefit out of the fact that the reply element is a BRC:

Please complete the card enclosed and drop it in the mail today.
It's already addressed. And the postage is paid.

6—*Minimize the buyer's risk and obligation.* Do whatever you can to minimize sales pressure on the prospect. If you follow up leads by phone instead of with the field sales force, say in your copy, "No salesperson will visit." If you do not follow up leads by phone, say, "No salesperson will call."

When offering anything free—a white paper, a webinar, even a brochure—say that it is free. Do not substitute the weaker "complimentary" when writing to a high-level business audience because you think "free" is not professional or will offend them. It won't.

Everybody wants free stuff, and businesspeople and professionals are no exception. A health care agency sent a direct mail piece inviting doctors to attend a symposium. They did an A/B split test of two versions; the only difference was that B offered a free pocket diary as a gift for attendance. Version B, offering the free gift, outpulled version A—with no free gift—sixfold. Busy doctors were persuaded to give up an afternoon by a free pocket diary that costs about a dollar!

Does the buyer have to agree to sit through a presentation or demonstration, or complete a survey? If he is not required to take further action once he accepts the offer, note this in your copy by saying: "There's no obligation . . . nothing to buy . . . and no commitment of any kind."

Sources and Resources

Bibliography

Abraham Group, The Compilation of Headlines.

Bly, Robert, The Copywriter's Handbook: Third Edition (Henry Holt & Co.).

Galletti, Carl, 2001, Greatest Headlines Ever Written (CarlGalleti.com).

Heimann, Jim, 40s All-American Ads (Taschen).

Masterson, Michael and John Force, Great Leads (AWAI).

Messner, Fred, Industrial Marketing (McGraw-Hill).

Schwab, Victor, How to Write a Good Advertisement (Echo Point Books).

Sugarman, Joe, The Adweek Copywriting Handbook (John Wiley & Sons).

Watkins, Julian, The 100 Greatest Advertisements (Dover).

E-newsletters

The Direct Response Letter
www.bly.com/reports

Courses

Accelerated Six-Figure Copywriting Course
www.awaionline.com

John Carlton's Simple Writing System.
https://simplewritingsystem.com/

Websites

AWAI
www.awailone.com

Bob Bly's website
www.bly.com

About the Author

Bob Bly has four decades of experience as a copywriter. McGraw-Hill calls Bob Bly "America's top copywriter." He has written copy for over one hundred clients including Kiplinger, Boardroom, Phillips, Agora, KCI, Nightingale-Conant, IBM, AT&T, and *Medical Economics.*

The author of more than ninety-five books, Bob's titles include *The Digital Marketing Handbook* (Entrepreneur Press) and *The New Email Revolution* (Skyhorse). He has published more than one hundred articles in *Amtrak Express, Cosmopolitan, Writer's Digest, DM News, New Jersey Monthly, City Paper, Chemical Engineering Progress,* and many other periodicals.

Bob writes a column for *Target Marketing,* a trade publication covering the direct marketing industry. *The Direct Response Letter,* Bob Bly's free e-newsletter, has over 65,000 subscribers.

Bob has given lectures on marketing, writing, and freelancing to numerous organizations including the Optical Society of America, Solutia, IBM, U.S. Army, Arco Chemical, Discover Card, and General Electric. He also taught writing at New York University.

He has won numerous awards including a Gold Echo from the Direct Marketing Association and an IMMY from the Information Industry

Association. Bob is a member of the Specialized Information Publishers Association and the American Institute of Chemical Engineers.

Bob Bly holds a B.S. in chemical engineering from the University of Rochester. Prior to becoming a full-time freelance copywriter in 1982, Bob was a technical writer for Westinghouse and advertising manager for Koch Engineering.

He can be reached at:

Bob Bly
31 Cheyenne Drive
Montville, NJ 07045
Phone: 973-263-0562
Fax 973-263-0613:
Email: rwbly@bly.com
Website: www.bly.com